بسم اللہ الرحمٰن الرحیم

CORRESPONDENCE
OF
SIR SYED AHMAD KHAN
AND HIS CONTEMPORARIES

Compiled and edited
by
Salim al-Din Quraishi

SANG-E-MEEL PUBLICATIONS
25-SHAHRAH-E-PAKISTAN (LOWER MALL) LAHORE

808.86 Correspondence of Sir Syed Ahmad
Khan and his — contempora —
ries : comp & ed. by salim —
al — Din Quraishi — Lahore :
Sang-e-Meel Publications, 1998.
155p.
1. Letter . I. Salim -al-Din
Qureshi.

1998
Published by :
NIAZ AHMAD
Sang-e-Meel Publications
Lahore

Rs. 200.00

ISBN 969 - 35 - 0865 - 3

Sang- e-Meel Publications
Chok Urdu Bazar Lahore. PAKISTAN. Phone : 7667970
Showroom : 25-Shahrah-e-Pakistan (Lower Mall),
Lahore. Pakistan. Phones: 7220100 - 7228143 fax : 7245101
Email lhr01660 @ paknet1. Ptc.pk http://www.sang-e-meel.com

Printed at : Combine Printers, Lahore.

TO

MY BROTHER

RIZWAN KALEEM

Introduction

According to Sir Syed's close friend and biographer, Altaf Husain Hali, Sir Syed knew very little English and yet we find a large number of his writings, correspondence and speeches in the English language. The fact is that although he could perhaps manage some polite conversation in English Sir Syed mostly depended on his friends, his son Syed Mahmud, or his secretary to translate his correspondence and speeches into English.

Hali gives an interesting insight on Sir Syed's speech-making:

> He would write short speeches in Urdu and then had them translated into English. He would then transcribe the text in Persian script so that he could read it as Urdu. His long speeches were read by the Secretary of the Council. On other occasions he delivered his speeches in Persian. [1]

Similarly his letters were either transcribed or typed by his secretary and later on signed by him in English.

So far only two collections of Sir Syed's English correspondence have been published, i.e.: Muhammad Ismail Panipati's *Letters to and from Sir Syed Ahmad Khan* (Lahore, 1993) and Safi Ahmad's *Selected documents from the Aligarh Archives*. Vol. 2. *Theodore Beck*. (Aligarh, 1988).

The present volume includes Sir Syed's correspondence with Sir Richard Temple, Sir Richard Strachey, Sir John Strachey and Sir William Muir as well as with the Viceroy, the Secretary of State, and the Governor of NWP. Also included here is the correspondence between the Viceroy, the Lieutenant-Governor of N.W.P and Oudh, Theodore Beck, Syed Mahmood, Maulavi Sami Ullah Khan and others regarding Sir Syed Ahmad Khan and the affairs of M.A.O. College.

The correspondence has been compiled from the following sources.

The Marquess of Lansdowne. Collection (BL.OIOC: MSS Eur.D 558/18.); Lord Elgin Collection (BL.OIOC: MSS Eur F 83-84); Sir Richard Temple Collection (BL.OIOC MSS Eur F 86/30); Sir Richard Strachey and Sir John Strachey Collection (BL.OIOC: MSS Eur. F 127); Muir Collection in the University of Edinburgh Library (Special Collection. Add. Muir. General 2021, folder 2, Letters relating to 1813-1902).

It is arranged under the following four subject headings:

1. Agitation against the Indian National Congress
2. Arab genealogy
3. Muslim University
4. Personal

The first part of this collection deals with Sir Syed's campaign in support of the Muslim petition to the House of Commons in which he had opposed the constitutional proposals put forward by the Indian National Congress.

His plea was "any system of proportionate representation would in no way protect Mahomedan interests, in as much as the Hindus of various races would be in a majority of four to one, and as all matters in the Council would be decided by a simple majority, the Mahomedan members would always be inevitably outvoted."

Another leading Muslim who helped Sir Syed in this campaign was Abdool Luteef, Secretary of the Mahomedan Literary Society, Calcutta. His correspondence on this issue is also included here.

Also included here is the correspondence of the Secretary of the Indian National Congress in support of its campaign as well as the text of a *Mahzar Namah* or an appeal in Urdu by over one hundred and fifty residents of Batala (both Hindus and Muslims) addressed to Sir Richard Temple informing him that their earlier petition in support of the proposals put forward by the Indian National Congress was signed by them on the false assurances given by Swami Ala Ram and his associates that it contained a request to the Government to excuse their taxes on cattle and land.

In the beginning Sir Syed had worked closely with Hindus in his educational activities but in 1867, while he was posted at Benares some leading Hindus of Benares decided to try to get the use of Urdu in Persian script discontinued in all the law courts and to have the use of Hindi in Devanagari script substituted for it.

Sir Syed would say that this was the first time that he felt sure "that the two nations will never be able to co-operate in any undertaking. At this time differences and enmity between them are small but thanks to the so-called educated classes, these feelings will progressively get worse as time passes."

Sir Syed's views were further strengthened by the attitude and statements of some of the most influential Hindus of his time. For example Raja Siva Prasad of Benares, who was a leading member of the Hindi lobby during one of his speeches in the Governor General's Legislative Council while assuring the British that "We Hindus do not consider the British as our conquerors. We not only acknowledge the divine right of our sovereigns, but find divinity in their persons." vehemently attacked the Muslims' treatment of their Hindu subjects:

> Let us see how the Muhammadans treated their conquered. They did not regard the Hindus even as men; hence to massacre them, to enslave their wives and daughters, to plunder their property, to demolish their temples, to deface the images, to force beef down their throats by violence, are the subjects which fill the so-called histories of the time. Even so good-natured a writer as Amir Khusrau was, alludes to the Hindus in such contemptuous terms as "raven faced" and " raven like" in nature (Ziq-ru va Zaqh Manish). The administration of the civil and criminal justice was completely in the hands of the Kazis, and no Hindu could possibly aspire to be a Kazi. No matter whether either or both parties were Muhammadans or Hindus, the judgement was invariably pronounced according to the Muhammadan Law or Sharia. The same Amir Khusrau

relates in his *Terikh-i Alai* that Ala-ud-din Khilji once sent for a Kazi and asked him what was written in the code of Muhammadan law regarding the Hindus. The Kazi answered that the " Hindus were zimmi (condemned to pay the jizya tax); if asked silver, they ought to pay gold with deep respect and humility; and if the collector of taxes were to fling dirt in their faces, they should gladly open their mouth wider. God's order is to keep them in subjection, and the Prophet enjoins on the Faithful to kill, plunder and imprison them, to make them Mussulmans or to put them to sword, to enslave them, and confiscate their property.

Akbar was the only Emperor who raised the Hindus and kept down the race distinction as low as he could, that was a matter of necessity. He had seen how his father was driven out from India. 2

One can imagine how Sir Syed would have felt sitting next to the Raja Sahib and listening to all these baseless accusations against the Muslim rule in India. In order to safeguard the "divine right" of his sovereigns the Raja Sahib later on joined hands with Sir Syed to oppose the Indian National Congress in forming the Indian Patriotic Association but soon afterwards he was to divide the members into two separate organisations, one Hindu and the other Muslim, each under the leadership of the respectivecommunity.

It is as a result of such experiences that Sir Syed became convinced that co-operation between the Hindus and the Muslims was not possible.

It is important to note that Sir Syed supported the first step toward self-government that Lord Ripon's Local Self-Government Bill represented and also highly approved the representative institutions which had made England 'great among the nations of the world'.

In fact, 'The principle of self-government by means of representative institutions is perhaps the greatest and noblest lesson which the beneficence of England will teach India'. But he asserted that:

> ...no part of India has yet arrived at the stage when the system of representation can be adopted, in its fullest scope, even in regard to local affairs...in borrowing from England the system of representative institutions, it is of the greatest importance to remember those socio-political matters in which India is distinguishable from England... India, a continent in itself, is inhabited by vast populations of different races and different creeds; the rigour of religious institutions has kept even neighbours apart; the system of caste is still dominant and powerful. In one and the same district the population may consist of various creeds and various nationalities...the system of representation means the representation of the views and interest of the majority of the population... So long as differences of race and creed and the distinction of caste form an important element in the .socio-political life of India, and influence her inhabitants in matters connected with the administration and welfare of the country at large, the system of election, pure and simple, cannot be safely adopted. The larger community would totally override the interests of the smaller community. 3

It was with these interests in mind that he launched his campaign against the election principles in the Indian Councils Bill put forward by the Indian National Congress. The appeal was supported by over 46,430 signatures from all parts of India. A similar appeal was launched by Abdool Lateef, Secretary of the Mohamadan Literary Society, Calcutta. While Sir Syed was sending his weekly despatches of signatures to Sir Richard Strachey, Abdool Lateef was addressing his mail to Sir John Gorst and Sir Richard Temple. The Indian National Congress had meanwhile opened an office in London under the guidance of Dadabhai Naroji to enlist the help of the Liberal and Radical members of the House of Commons. At the same time various committees of the Indian National Congress in India were regularly sending their submissions in support of the bill to Richard Temple.

The Muhammadan petition was presented to the Parliament by Sir Richard Temple. Speaking during the debate on the Indian Councils

Act (1861) Amendment Bill on 28 March 1892 in the House of Commons he put forward the Muslim case in the following words:

> The Mahomedans say that they would be outvoted by the Hindoos in every place, and they naturally wish to maintain some influence in the country, whose destinies in historic times they have so largely helped to mould. They ask in effect, that there should be some arrangement for the proper representation of their important minority, which may now be numbered at between 50,000,000 and 60,000,000. 4

The Prime Minister and Secretary of State for Foreign Affairs, The Marquess of Salisbury explained to Parliament the hostile attitude of one community in India against the other and the difficulties he faced in recommending the introduction of a representative government in India.

> Representative Government answers admirably so long all those who are represented desire much the same thing, and have interest tolerably analogous; but it is put to an intolerable strain when it rests upon a community divided into two sections, one of which is bitterly hostile to other, and desirous of opposing it upon all occasions. We do not know how the Mahomedan and Hindoo populations if placed face to face with each other in elective representative Government would view each other; but we know, at all events, that one of the heaviest responsibility and severest duties of the Government of India is to prevent the outbreak of hostilities caused by the profound difference between these two communities - differences in race, traditions, history, and creed. These are some among the difficulties; and there is another difficulty.... and that is, that if you want to have the elective principle of government, the first thing you have to find before you advance a single step upon your journey is a constituency; and a constituency is that which we are at present entirely without. We have been offered as a constituency for the representation of the warlike races of the Punjaub, the aristocratic people of

> Rajpootana, and for the vast population of the ryots, spread over the whole of India, a body elected only for the purpose of making streets and taking care of drains....5

As a result of these efforts "A Bill to make better provision for the Constitution of the Council of the Governor General of India and for amending the Legislative Councils of the several Presidencies and Provinces of India by enlarging their number, constituting them on partial Elective basis, and increasing their powers." was passed by Parliament in 1892.

The second part of the volume deals with Sir Syed's correspondence with Sir John Strachey and Sir Richard Temple regarding Arab genealogy. We also learn his views on the advent of Mahdi: "I am glad to tell you that all traditions relating to the advent of Mahdi towards the end of the world are quite groundless and false".

The third part of the collection is mainly about the management of the Aligarh College and includes detailed reports on the activities of the College and various crises it faced during its earlier years. The progress of the College was carefully monitored by the authorities who kept the Viceroy abreast of all developments. In one of these reports he was informed:

> The Mahomedans interested in the Institution are divided into two parties. One part, headed by Sir Syud Ahmed, was (and is) in favour of education on English lines, and of liberal principles in religion. The other part is headed by Maulvie Samiulla Khan, ...is, or professes to be an orthodox Mahomedan, and is not in favour of the liberal policy of Sir Syud.

The College was going through a very difficult phase after over one and a half lakh of rupees were embezzled by Sham Bihari Lal, a Head Clerk in Sir Syed's office. While this was happening his son, Syed Mahmud was " going from bad to worse through drink."

Soon after the death of his father Syed Mahmud took over the whole management of the College and as Life Secretary of the College it was " practically impossible ... to get rid of Mr Mahmud ".

The difficulty was resolved by tremendous efforts on the parts of Nawab Mohsin-ul-Mulk and Maulavi Sami Ullah Khan. It is through their efforts that the "financial safety of the College" was assured when the Nawab of Rampur agreed to give a donation of Rs 50,000 and increased the monthly grant from Rs 100 to 200.

The last part of the volume deals with Sir Syed's efforts in securing Syed Mahmud's appointment in Allahabad High Court as a Judge. The correspondence also reveals the Viceroy's concern about the visit of a Turkish envoy to India and his efforts, through Sir Syed Ahmad Khan, to find out the true nature of the envoy's visit as well as any information regarding Turkey's involvement in the political affairs of the region.

The appendix contains the full text of Sir Syed's petition to the House of Commons.

The biographical notes given at the end of the work provide short biographies of the principal characters mentioned in the correspondence.

In coclusion I must thank my friend Dr Avril Powell of the School of Oriental and African Studies, University of London for providing me with the reference to Sir Syed's letters to Sir William Muir at Edinburgh University; and my daughter, Rukhsana and my wife Maryam (Margarita Maura) for helping me to type the text and go through the proofs.

Salim al-Din Quraishi

23 December, 1997

References:

1. Hayat-i javed, by Altaf Husain Hali. Lahore, Academy Punjab, 1957. p. 286.
2. Criminal Procedure Code, 1882, Amendment. Abstract of the Proceedings of the Council of the Governor-General of India Assembled for the Purpose of Making Laws and Regulations, 1883. BL: OIOC/V/9/9. pp. 199-201)
3. For full text of Sir Syed's speech *See* R. Coupland, The Indian Problem, 1833-1935. London, 1942. p. 154
4. Debates, Questions etc. on Indian Affairs. Indian Councils Amendment Act, 1890. March 6 1890. BL: OIOC V/3/1593.
5. Ibid.

Contents

2. ARAB GENEALOGY

3. ALIGARH UNIVERSITY

3. PERSONAL

AGITATION

AGAINST THE

INDIAN NATIONAL CONGRESS

1

16, Toltollah,
Calcutta.
22 April, 1890

Honoured Sir,
By the mail of the 1st instant, the Committee of the Mahomedan Literary Society of Calcutta have forwarded a petition to the Honourable House of Commons protesting against the apprehended endeavour of the so called National Congress Party to procure a recognition of the elective system in the Indian Councils Bill now under discussion.

We have not considered it necessary to get our petition largely signed by the Mahomedans because, in the first place, it would have caused a great deal of delay, whereby the petition might have reached parliament too late; and secondly however largely we might have secured Mahomedan signatures they would have been but a drop in the ocean, as compared with the Hindoos - who have already forwarded and are forwarding hundreds of numerously signed memorials from all parts of India in support of the elective principle.

Our sole reliance is in the justice of our cause, as is well known to all those English gentlemen who have studied the subject and taken an impartial view of the question.

As no one knows of the deplorable condition of the Mahomedans of India then your Honour, and as your Honour has always taken the greatest interest in the welfare of our community, we look up to your honour and to your friends to support us in this crisis.

Sincerely trusting this may find your Honour and Lady Temple in the enjoyment of perfect health.

I beg to remain your Honours most respectfully,

Abdool Luteef

2

The Congress Committee Office
100, Mount Road,
Madras.
7 May, 1890

To: Sir Richard Temple
Member of Parliament,
London.

Honourable Sir,
I have much pleasure in forwarding by to-day's mail, a petition to be presented to the Honourable Members of the House of Commons with about 700 signatures from the residents of Bellary regarding the reforms of the Indian Legislative Council.

On behalf of the Madras Standing Congress Committee and of the petitioners I request you will be pleased to present the petition to the Honourable House and give your support to the prayer of the memorialists.

I am,

Yours truly

N. Viraraghavacharia
Honorary Secretary to the Congress Committee

3

M. A. O. College,
Aligarh,
13 May, 1890.

Dear Gen. Strachey,
I have the pleasure to send you 4132 signatures of the petition. The most marked feature about them consists of a total 563 from 5 towns in Sind.

The places from which these particular signatures have been obtained are as follows:

Fatehgarh	87
Ajmer	435
Dinapore (B)	86
Faridabad (P)	26
Batala (P)	397
Denagpur (P)	184
Shahjehanpore	291
Rungpur (Bengal)	164
Lucknow	136
Agra	56
Moradabad	147
Dindigul (Madras)	63
Baghlampur(P)	63
Patna (B)	51
Mymensingh (B)	128
Karachi (Sind)	130
Hyderabad (Sind)	248
Sukkur(Sind)	81
Larkana (Sind)	124
Tatta(Sind)	18
Sherkot	131
Ajmer	112
Calcutta	167
Karnal(P)	169
Indore	83
Chafna	9
Bulandshahr	79
Jaunpur	119
Total	**4132**

I enclose a curious piece of paper that was attached to the Batala Signatures. A translation of it is as follows:

We the undersigned inhabitants of Batala who have signed this paper signed a petition brought round by Swami Ala Ram which was stated to contain a request that the Government would excuse the taxes especially those on cattle. Swami Ala Ram and his coadjutors told us that the object of the petition was the remittance of taxation. We are all of us quite opposed to the proposals of the National Congress and very gladly sign this petition.

150 names are appended. I have not sent a sheet containing them.

I think the wider area from which signatures came streaming in is worthy of note.

The total number of signatures of our petition is now **38,173**

I remain

Yours very truly

Theodore Beck

4

The Congress Committee Office,
100, Mount Road,
Madras,
14 May, 1890

To: Sir Richard Temple,
Member of Parliament,
London.

Honourable Sir,
I have much pleasure in forwarding by to-day's mail, a petition to be presented to the Honourable Members of the House of Commons with about 336 signatures from the residents of Ellore regarding the reforms of the Indian Legislative Council

On behalf of the Madras Standing Congress Committee and of the petitioners I request you will be pleased to present the petition to the Honourable House and give your support to the prayer of the memorialists.

I am,
Yours truly

N. Viraraghavacharia
Honorary Secretary to the Congress Committee

5

To:
The Right Honourable Sir Richard Temple,
K.C.S.I M.P. Bart
16 Toltollah,
Calcutta.
20 May, 1890

Honoured Sir,
On the 22 ultimo I have addressed a letter to your Honour informing you of our having forwarded a petition to the Honourable House of Commons, protesting on behalf of the Mahomedan Community, against the apprehended recognition of the elective principle in the Indian Councils Bill.

Our petition was sent to the Right Honourable Sir John E.Gorst for presenting to Parliament and from his letter received by the last mail, we are much gratified to learn that your Honour has kindly undertaken to lay it on the table - as we are certain that our case could not be placed in better hands.

Please accept our most grateful thanks for this kindness shown to the Mahomedans of India.

Sincerely trusting that this may find your Honour and Lady Temple in the perfect enjoyment of health.

I beg to remain your Honours most respectfully,

Abdool Luteef

6

Standing Congress Committee Office,
Allahabad,
May 21,1890

To: Sir Richard Temple Bart. G.C.S.I
M.P.
London

Sir,
I have taken this liberty to forward it to you nine petitions of the residents of Allahabad containing 6,817 signatures for presentation to the Honourable the House of Commons. I have been encouraged to encroach upon your valuable time by the knowledge that the programme of the Indian National Congress is in full accord with your own views on the question of the reforms and expansion of various Legislative Councils of India. The lecture delivered by you at a meeting of the East India Association in August last and before our scheme was completed at the last session of the Indian National Congress held in Bombay in December 1889, runs as far as it relates to the Indian Councils so closely on the lines of our programme, as to assure us that you will be pleased not only to present the petitions to Parliament, but to add to them the weight of your most valuable support. If a distinguished and experienced statesman like yourself

could see no objection to confer on our countrymen the privilege of election to the limited extent to which we claim it, there appears to be absolutely no reason why even the most cautious member of either of the two great political parties in England should hesitate to grant this most moderate demand of the people of India.

I respectfully beg to assure you, Sir, that the members of the Reform Party in the country are most anxious not to make Indian subjects party questions in Parliament

We value the support of the Conservative as highly as that of the Liberals and nothing can give us great satisfaction than a conviction that the people of England whatever differences there might be in their opinions about purely English political questions, take an equal interest in the welfare of India. We look to you Sir, with great confidence for protecting us against the attacks of those thoughtless people who most unjustly and unwisely charge our party with disloyalty to the British Crown. The greatest praise which can be bestowed upon the English nation is this: that they have been and are doing their best to raise us to their own standard of civilisation, and are desirous to allow us participate, so far as may be practicable, in their own fine institutions.

We must be idiots or lunatics to be disloyal to the rule of such a nation and yet we are charged with disloyalty. Loyal to the backbone, we naturally very much resent this most unfounded charge. And we look to Honourable members like your goodself who combine large and varied Indian experience with great statesmanship, to remove the effect of such misrepresentation from the minds of Honourable House. The mother of parliaments, when once assured of our loyalty which is of course unquestionable will no doubt grant our prayer.

I have the honour to be
Sir,

Yours most obedient Servant

Ajoodhia Nath Pundit
President Allahabad Standing Congress Committee

7

Aligarh,
27 May, 1890.

Dear Gen. Strachey,
I am sending you by this mail 1998 signatures of the Mahomedan's petition against the Congress. The total number of signatures is now 41859. The signatures I am sending you have come from the following places:

Places	No of signatures
Vizianagram	283
Covinbatore	58
Shikarpore	270
Jihanabad	71
Hariana	87
Allahabad	174
Shahjehanpore	83
Ferozepore	748
Memansingh	124
Total	**1998**

I learn from the papers that Sir Richard Temple has laid before the Parliament the humble petition of the Indian Mahomedans and I myself and on behalf of the Mahomedans thank you and Sir Richard very much for this act of kindness and sympathy.

With my best compliments.

I remain,

Yours very truly

Syud Ahmed

8

To: The Right Honourable,
Sir Richard Temple, G.C.S.I. M.P. Bart

16 Toltollah,
Calcutta.
10 June, 1890

Honoured Sir,
Since my last letter addressed to your Honour on the 20th ultimo I have received a letter from the Right Honourable Sir John Gorst, from which I have been much gratified to learn that your Honour has been pleased to mention him about my humble self and the Mahomedan Literary Society in extremely kind terms.

We have also been very glad to find that our petition has been presented to the Honourable House by your Honour' and we are confident that when the time comes you will support our prayer, and save us from the misfortune with which we are threatened.

Sincerely trusting that this may find your Honour and Lady Temple in the enjoyment of perfect health.

I beg to remain

Your Honours most respectfully,

Abdool Luteef

9

Aligarh,
24th June, 1890.

Dear General Strachey,
I am sending you by this mail 1270 signatures on the Mahomedan petition against the Congress.

The total number of signatures is now 48,651. The signatures I am now sending you have come from the following places:

Places	**No of signatures**
Faridpur Bengal	245
Akola	59
Meymensigh	544
Shahjehanpur	212
Jaunpore	210
Total	**1270**

With my best compliments.

I am,

Yours very truly

Syed Ahmad

10

To: Sir Richard Temple, K.C.S.I, M.P.
London

From: Standing Congress Committee Office,
Allahabad.
June 25,1890

Sir,
In continuation of my letter no 254 dated the 21st of May 1890 I beg to intimate that the petition signed by 2160 residents of the town and districts of Allahabad have been despatched to your address by today's mail. The favour of your presenting them to the Honourable the House of Commons is solicited.

I have the honour to be,

Sir,

Yours most obedient servant

Ajoodhia Nath Pundit
President of the Standing Congress Committee,
Allahabad

11

69, Lancaster Gate,
W.
2 July, 1890

My Dear Temple,
By every mail since I sent you the Mahometan petition I have been receiving additional signatures which I presume must now be

disregarded from a formal point of view, though they are of course quite as important in fact as those attached to the petition when it was presented.

On the 29th April the numbers of signatures despatched was 26,846. On the 6th May it had increased to 34,041. The next week it became 38,173, then 39,867, then 41,865, next 44,523 and by the last mail which came in yesterday it is announced to have risen to 46,430.

Although I fear they may not be received by the House I venture to send you the packets of signatures to show that the feeling of those who continue to forward them from India is unabated in its strength and that the prayer of the petition is supported from all parts of India. The names of the places from which these signatures came, including:

Bombay, Madras, Vizianagram, Coimbatore, Shikarpore, Midnapoor, Sukkur, Larkhana, Chitagong, Maimansingh, Jhelum, Calcutta, Lucknow; Ajmer, Kurnal.

Besides a great number of towns and districts in the North Western Provinces of which special note need not be taken as the petition originated with the Mahomedans of that region.

I enclose for you pursual one of the letters I received from Sir Syed Ahmed Khan in which he thanks you for having presented the petition.

I also enclose a letter from Mr Beck, Sir Syed Ahmad's Secretary which (sic) sent me a paper also enclosed signed by 150 persons resident of Batala in the Punjab describing how the petition in favour of the proposals of the National Congress was put before them and the true nature of those proposals misrepresented.

I have delayed giving you this information until I saw that it was likely that the Indian Council Bill would be gone in with.
Yours sincerely

R. Strachey

12

محضرنامہ

ہم باشندگان بٹالہ میں سے جس جس شخص نے اس عرضداشت پر جو سوامی آلارام صاحب الٰہ آبادی باشندہ سے پیش کی ہے دستخط کئے ہیں صرف اس مضمون پر کئے ہیں۔ کہ گورنمنٹ عالیہ سے ٹیکس کی معافی خصوصاً کابلی ٹیکس کی معافی کرائی جائے۔ اور ہم پر سوامی آلارام صاحب الٰہ آبادی۔ اور انکے معاونین نے یہ ظاہر کیا ہے۔ کہ ٹیکس کی معافی کی یہ عرضداشت ہے۔ ہم سب لوگ نیشنل کانگرس کے اغراض سے ہرگز متفق نہیں ہیں۔ اور ہم خوشی سے اس محضرنامہ پر دستخط کرتے ہیں۔ ۳۰ اپریل سنہ ۱۸۹۰

العبد [illegible] — العبد مفتی غلام حسین — العبد اللہ [illegible] — العبد شیخ فضل دین — العبد جان محمد

العبد عبد الصمد — العبد غلام [illegible] — العبد [illegible] — العبد مبارک علی — العبد امام الدین

العبد صدرالدین — العبد عطا محمد — العبد حکم دین — فتح دین — فقیر — پیر بخش — العبد

میراں بخش — وزیر علی — پیر بخش — العبد حسن [illegible]

[illegible] — محکم دین — خیر الدین — امام دین — العبد محمد شریف

العبد فضل الدین — العبد حسین بخش — العبد چراغ الدین

العبد [illegible] — العبد غلام محمد — العبد فضل دین — العبد [illegible]

حسن بخش — نظام الدین — فضل الدین — قمر الدین — [illegible] — نور محمد

[illegible] — [illegible] — [illegible] — منیر محمد

ARAB GENEALOGY

13

1, Marloes Road,
Kensington.
Sunday

Dear Sir John Strachey,
Many thanks for your kindness in sending the information. Professor Robertson Smith tells me he thinks the whale is a late addition to the tribal beasts but he did not give his reasons. I hope Syed Ahmed Khan will not think it disagreeable to find the correspondence with red.

Sincerely yours

A. lang

14

1, Marloes Road,
Kensington.
Tuesday.

Dear Sir John Strachey,
I have my eyes on the animals: these I see are all common in Arabia['s] West district but I am not sure of the Whale.

The things desirable to know are:

1. Whether Sir John's informant knows if they have any story as to why they have animal emblem? (The ordinary tale claims descent from "Totem")

2. Whether members of a tribe have any scruples about eating the animal which is their crest? (most of those on the box are not edible brutes, just as the animals the Jews might not eat were those few people would care to partake of)

3. May a man of the whale or any other crest marry a girl of the same crest, and if he may now is there any tradition of a time when he might not?

If Sir John Strachey could find out the answers to these questions, they would be of considerable value to anthropologists.

The only article on Semitic Totems is Robertson Smith's in the *Journal of Philosophy*. I don't think he knew that animal clans still existed in India

Yours very truly

A.Lang

15

Aligarh,
13 August, 1881

My Dear Sir John,
I hope you have received my last letter. I now write to enclose a brief description of the engraving on the casket presented to you by the College. I delayed sending it to you as I wished to send a brief history of the various tribes, but on reconsideration I think it is unnecessary for understanding the symbolical idea of the engraving. I hope what I have written is intelligible enough to explain the symbolical engraving. It will interest you to hear that the money which you have kindly sent to the College from an anonymous friend, will be employed in building one set of rooms for the resident students of the College. In order to secure the benefit of good example the committee propose to put up an inscription in the room to the effect that it was

constructed with the donation of an English gentleman who has not told his name to the College Committee.

The room will bring an income of Rs. 120/ per annum to the College, being the rent of the room payable by the student who lives in it.

My son, Syed Mahmood has gone to Hyderabad by order of the Government of India. Under the present arrangement he is to stay there for a year but it is likely he may have to stay longer.

I hope both you and Lady Strachey are in the enjoyment of good health. You know how much pleasure it is to me and my family to hear of your welfare. Please give my best respect to Lady Strachey and tell her that we are waiting to hear what arrangement she proposes to make about the portrait of yourself in regard to which I wrote to you in my last.

With feelings of sincere gratitude and respect.

Always yours sincerely,

Syed Ahmed.

16

To:
Sir John Strachey,
G.C.S.I

Aligarh,
8 April, 1884

My Dear Sir John,
I have to thank you very much for your favour of the 22nd February; enclosing copy of a drawing from an old American sculpture. I do not

think whether it was the work of the old Arabs of representing the unanimity of heart and speech by drawing lines from each animal's heart and tongue, but I am rather inclined to think it was not their custom.

It is a long time when I had also seen the old American painting a drawing of which Mr Lang gave you, and when I was making a sketch of the box it ocurred to me that it would be nicer if the symbols of the Arabs tribes were inscribed on it instead of ordinary flower engravings and it would better express the sense of gratitude and thanks if the lines were drawn from each of the animals tongue instead of eyes.

I doubt whether the animals in the old American paintings are symbols of tribes. When I saw it I thought the artist's idea was that "all the animals of air, water and earth and those living under the earth as well as all men were anxiously waiting and looking out for your arrival"; and hence the lines were drawn from their eyes; and as the painting contains a figure of man also, it cannot be supposed that the animals are symbolical of tribes. The animals represent[ed] on the box were not themselves the symbols of tribes, but the names of those animals were the names of the ancestors of various tribes that made the figures of those animals on the box.

The members of a tribe would have no scruple in eating the animals whose name denoted their tribe. Neither the marriage between the males and females of the tribes of the same name was forbidden.; they married among themselves as well as among the members of other tribes.

The Bedouin Arabs of this day also denote their tribes by the same manner.

You will be interested to learn that the Mahdi of Soudan belongs to the tribes of "Kelb" or the tribe represented by Dog. I do not recollect whether this tribe is also represented or not on the box.

The Indian Mahomedans have no such tribe names. Only the Mahomedans of 12 towns of Sayyids in Mozaffarnaggar district have adopted the various tribes names which are the names of animals, as well as other names; but I could not ascertain why they adopted these names. Sometime ago when I wanted to ascertain and enquired of them then reason of this, but they could not give me a satisfactory or reliable answer.

I thought that perhaps they had adopted the names of those Arab tribes of old from which they were descended but I found that this fact also did not agree; for if they were really Sayyids as they claim themselves to be they could not belong to any other tribe except Kurresh while none of them bears the name of that tribe.

You will be glad to hear that Syed Mahmood has gone into High Court. At first he was gazetted to officiate for Mr Justice Zyrrell who has gone on a years furlough, but afterwards the notification was modified and he was gazetted to officiate for Mr Justice Straight who is now acting as the Chief Justice. And probably the new Chief Justice will arrive in November when Mr Straight will revert to his post and Syed Mahmood will have to go back to his substantial post.

I was really much pleased to hear that your portrait was nearly finished and the more so because Lady Strachey approved of it. I have sent to you 105 Pounds through Messers Henry S. King and Co. which I trust will reach you in time.

I request you and Lady Strachey to be good enough to have it mounted in a good frame and let me know the cost which I shall remit in time.

I am glad to tell you that the College is getting on very well. In the Budget for this year the income has been estimated at Rs. 48,115-2-6 and the expenditure is estimated at Rs. 47,775-6-0. Sir Alfred Lyall having been pleased to raise the amount of the government part to Rs. 12,000 a year. The building expense was nothing to do with the above estimates as the building fund is quite apart from it.

The College now teaches upto the B.A. standard of the Calcutta University and at the last University examinations two students from this College passed the B.A. Examination and a good lot passed the University examinations.

The Committee has proposed to increase the dimensions of the Strachey Hall and now it will become 20 feet longer that at first planned.

Moreover, it will have a gallery on three sides while on the fourth your portrait will be hung up after me.

The new plans are being prepared and as soon as they are ready the committee will begin the building work of the Stratchey Hall.

Mr Wilfred Blunt was here some time ago. Our Committee is quite opposed to his views which he expressed in his lectures at various places; for our Committee has decided that no good or benefit can be derived by the revival of the old Asiatic sciences and arts. The bigoted Mahomedans like his views very much; but those who understand these matters do not agree with him.

So far as I know the Indian Mahomedans are not interested in the Mahdi of Soudan and I am glad to tell you that all traditions relating to the advent of the Mahdi towards the end of the world are quite groundless and false.

Last year I wrote a powerful article proving that all these traditions were unfounded and false and there was no such thing to come as the appearance of the Mahdi.

In my last tour into the Panjab I was pleased to see that hundreds of Punjab Mohomedans agreed with the views of my article; however the common people believe that a Mahdi will be born towards the end of the world.

With kindest regards for Lady Strachey,

I remain,

Yours sincerely

Syed Ahmed

P.S. I return back the sketch of the painting

17

The engraving on the basket presented by the Mohamedan Anglo Oriental College Committee to Sir John Strachey G.C.S.I represents 12 different animals. Each animal is the symbol of each of the 12 principal tribes of the Arabs from whom the principal Mohamedan families of India are descended. The names of the each of the 12 tribes are words signifying the various animals. In the engraving each of the animal is numbered thus:

1. Anas (Eagle)
2. Khazaraj (lion)
3. Bakr (camel)
4. Namr (leopard)
5. Bughail (mule)
6. Ghanam (sheep)
7. Kilab (dog)
8. Zirad (monkey)
9. Aus (wolf)
10. Dubb (lizard)
11. Rakkash (snake)
12. Qoraish (Whale)

Of these tribes the Quraish or the whale tribe was the most important and powerful - they were the Princes of Mecca before Islam. The Prophet Mahomed himself was descended from that tribe and all Sayyads or descendants of the Prophet and descendants of his principal associates therefore belong to the Qoraish tribe. The principal founders of the Mohomedan Anglo Oriental College are descended from the Prophet and his Associates and therefore belong to the Qoraish tribe.

In the engraving lines drawn from the hearts and tongues of the whale, represent that all Mohomedans are unanimous in heart and speech in expressing their feelings of gratitude to Sir John Strachey through the mouth of their leader the Qoraish or the whale.

ALIGARH UNIVERSITY

18

Benares
June 2nd, 1876

Respected Sir,
I have been much flattered by your very kind note of the 26 ultimo. A copy of the prospectus enclosed with your letter had reached me a few days before and I had it published in the Aligarh Scientific Society Gazette with an Urdoo version. One copy of the prospectus with its translation as published in the S. Gazette has been sent to H.H. the Nawab of Rampur who I am sure will patronize the work. It is indeed one of the old and well known Arabic works and it will give me great pleasure to secure assistance from my friends towards its publication. I shall try my best to have at least 10 copies sold.

The people of the N.W. Provinces are being informed by and by of your intentions to leave India after the rains, and those to whom the information has reached are thinking of the means come to express their feelings of gratitude to you in return of the favours you have conferred upon them and also their feeling of sorrow and regret at your departure from this country which will beyond doubt be felt throughout these provinces and more particularly by us who had the honour of enjoying your special favour. It is true that you will continue to have the same kind regards for us and will always keep us informed of your welfare but we shall at last lose the pleasure of meeting you frequently.

You must have heard that I have already tendered my application for permission to retire from service.

I shall give up work in the middle of July and shall proceed to Aligarh because I see that the College work can not be accomplished without my presence on the spot. So I shall be at Aligarh at the time you will come down the hills. I wish therefore you could stop for a short time at Aligarh on your way to Calcutta, and I shall be highly thankful to you if you will be good enough to make previous arrangements for your stay at Aligarh for a short time and favour me with information before hand.

I am yours respectfully

Syed Ahmed

To: Honble Sir W. Muir, K.C.S.I

19

Hon'ble S.W. Muir, K.C.S.I

Benares
July 6, 1876

Respected Sir,
In the meeting which was lately held at Benares it was proposed, rather was finally decided to have a statue made in order to preserve the memory of your kindness to the country. Though one or two Mahomedans may have joined in this proposal, yet as I believe, you are well aware that the Mahomedan community in general can hardly take any part in it. The members of our committee are therefore desirous of having separate ceremonial of your favours established in their College. It is their intention to found one or two scholarships in your name for the study of Arabic language of which you are well known throughout the country to be a good scholar, and also to erect a small handsome house for recreation upon the Park with your name inscribed upon the same. The accomplishment of the latter part of the proposal however depends upon the sufficiency or otherwise of the amount of subscriptions raised and I doubt whether we shall be able to collect a sum which will be sufficient for the scholarships as well as for the building.

If you can conveniently stay for a few hours at Aligarh on your way down from the hills the committee could commence a meeting on the day you arrive there in order to present you a farewell address written in the Arabic language. In the same address they could ask your permission to found a scholarship in your name. But if you could not manage to stay at Aligarh College I could present the address to you through a deputation on their behalf at Allahabad where you are to stop for a day at least. I therefore most respectfully solicit the favour of your kindly informing me of your wishes in this matter so that we may at once commence work.

I will retire from public service on the 15th inst. and will proceed direct to Aligarh.

I remain yours respectfully,
Syed Ahmed

To: Honble Sir W. Muir K.C.S.I

20

Programme of Proceedings to be observed on the arrival of the

Hon'ble Sir John Strachey, G.C.S.I.,C.I.E,

Visitor Of the Muhammadan Anglo-Oriental

College at Aligarh

The Honourable Sir John Strachey will arrive at Aligarh on Friday, the 10th December, 1880, at 4.52 P.M. Mr Siddons, the Principal of the College; Mr Nesbitt, the Head Master; Kunwar Muhammad Lutf Ali Khan, President, College Fund Committee, Maulvi Sayyad Fariduddin Ahmad Khan Bahadur, President; Maulvi Muhammad Sami Ullah Khan Bahadur; Khwajah Muhammad Yusuf and Sayyad Ahmad Khan, Secretaries of the Managing Committee and Sayyad Zuhur Husain and Muhammad Mustafa Khan, Rais of Burhagaon, Members of the Committee will receive him at the Railway Station.

The Honourable Sir John Strachey will, with his party, drive from the Station to the house of Sayyad Ahmad Khan, accompanied by Sayyad Ahmad Khan and the President of the College Fund Committee. On reaching the house the President will withdraw.

On Saturday, the 11th December, at 12 of the noon, an address will be presented to him on behalf of the College Fund Committee, and a meeting will be held for the purpose at the place known by the name of Strachey Hall, which is now in the course of construction.

The procession to the scene of the presentation of the address will consist of the following gentlemen, the first of whom will accompany the Honourable Sir John from Sayyad Ahmad Khan's house, while the rest will receive him at the stairs of the Strachey Hall.

Kunwar Muhammad Lutf Ali Khan, President, College Fund Committee.

Maulvi Sayyad Fariduddin Ahmad Khan Bahadur, President Managing Committee.

Raja Jaikishandas Bahadur, C.S.I Member, Managing Committee.

Sayyad Zuhur Husain.

Maulvi Muhammad Sami Ullah Khan Bahadur.

Sayyad Muhammad Mahmud Esquire.

Maulvi Sayyad Zain-ul-Abudin Khan.

Maulvi Muhammad Karim.

Muhammad Inayatullah Khan of Bhikampur.

Muhammad Abdushshakaur Khan of Bhikampur

Muhammad Mustafa Khan of Burhagaon.

Muhammad Masud Ali Khan of Danpur.

Muhammad Zafaryab Khan.

Khwajah Muhammad Ismail.

Munshi Muhammad Mushtak Husain.

Maulvi Khwajah Muhammad Yusuf.

Sayyad Ahmad Khan.

All except the Honourable Sir John Strachey and those who accompany him are expected to be in their seats before his arrival.

The whole assembly will rise as the Honourable Sir John Strachey enters, and will remain so until he is seated.

Maulvi Sayyad Fariduddin Ahmad Khan, Bahadur, stepping forward will, then, on behalf of the Committee, request the Honourable Sir John Strachey's permission that an address may be presented and may be read by Sayyad Muhammad Mahmud, Esquire, in English and an Urdu translation of it by Munshi Mushtak Husain.

On the Honourable Sir John Strachey's intimating his pleasure to receive the address it will be read in both the languages and afterwards presented in a silver casket to the Honourable Sir John Strachey by Kunwar Muhammad Lutf Ali Khan, President, College Fund Committee.

During the Honourable Sir John Strachey's reply all the assembly will remain seated, and at its conclusion Sayyad Ahmad Khan will introduce Agha Husain, a student of the College, who has won the Strachey Medal this year, and will request the Honourable Sir John Strachey to award the medal with his own hands.

Maulvi Muhammad Sami Ullah Khan will, then on behalf of the Committee, thank Sir John Strachey and Lady Strachey.

Sir John Strachey will then rise and will be conducted to his carriage with the same honours as those with which he was received.

After this Sir John Strachey will inspect the new building for the College, the new Boarding House etc.

At 5 P.M. Sir John Strachey will proceed to the Railway Station, and there the same gentlemen who received him on the day previous, will be present.

Aligarh
The 24th November, 1880

Syed Ahmed
Secretary, M.A.O.College Fund Committee

21

To: Hon'ble Sir John Strachey, G.C.S.I.,C.I.E.

Honourable Sir,
We, the members of the Muhammadan Anglo-Oriental College Fund Committee, approach you on this occasion, on behalf of our community, to give expression to feelings of sincere gratitude, which we entertain towards you, for the countenance and support with which you have honoured our endeavours.

You, Sir, are aware that of all the races inhabiting the continent of India, and doing homage to the British Throne, there is non which has remained so far behind the age as the Musalman subjects of the Empress of India. They have withstood the influence of the age with an apathy calculated to bring in its train the worst evils of social and political degradation. A complication of social causes has given birth to the danger to which we allude. But whilst fully aware of the danger before us, we are cheered with the feeling, that neither our history of the past, nor our present position under the British rule, warrants the fears which we, in our solicitude, are apt to entertain about the future of our races in India.

Whilst some of our countrymen have devoted their energies to agitating political grievances, supposed or real, we, an humble body of Her Majesty's subjects, have never forgotten the truth which underlies the proverbial saying - that to deserve is essential before desiring anything. We have been guided by a deep-seated conviction that our only chance of success under the British rule lies in education; that we can never hope to discharge our duties as citizens of a civilized State without acquiring the intellectual training necessary for a proper intelligence of the principles upon which the government under which we live is conducted. Our principle object has been to increase amongst our co-religionists the means of acquiring the education necessary alike for being useful members of society and for being good subjects of a civilized rule. We are proud as a desire to advance our own national interests.

The establishment of the Muhammadan Anglo-Oriental College is the outcome of our humble endeavours, - the embodiment of our national aspirations in the direction to which we alluded. The scheme which brought about the establishment of the College began in a movement which, during the last few years, has been gaining strength, and which, we are convinced, is destined to produce greater effects upon our national position than might at first be supposed. Education, in the sense in which the present generation understands the term, has had limited scope in India. Everything that has hitherto been done, has been done almost entirely by the State. But the time has arrived when the people of the country must begin to feel that the state, though the natural guardian of our interests, must not be regarded as the only supporter of educational institutions. It has been our earnest endeavour to impress upon our co-religionists the great truth, that the education is as much a necessity of civilized citizenship as other circumstances which contribute to advance human happiness, and that the State can no more be expected to be the only source of supplying this necessity, than it can be expected to provide from the public revenues the subsistence of all its subjects.

Animated with these feelings, we began to give a practical effect to our views. It seems to be the inevitable lot of all the movements which have for their aim the removal of long-established evils, to meet with opposition, and our humble endeavours have not been an exception to the general rule. We had to contend with obstinate bigotry and prejudices on the one hand, and lethargic indifference and want of enthusiasm on then other. Our success, however was greater than we expected. But at one point of our efforts we felt that all we had succeeded in achieving would be lost in one blow. We had fallen out of sympathy with the local authorities of the district, our motives were misunderstood, our efforts were derided as ephemeral, we had failed to win that which in a country like India is the greatest source of encouragement, - the good-will and sympathy of those who were the immediate representatives of Government in this district. That was a danger, the greatness of which can be understood only by those who are familiar with the condition which govern the socio-political life of the natives of India. That was the most critical period in the history of the College. Happily for ourselves, and for the interest of the Muhammadan education in this part of India, you, Sir, were the head of the Government of these provinces - and we were saved from the danger to which we have alluded, and with which we confess we had felt ourselves unable to cope. We had the good fortune to win your private and public sympathy; you condescended to take interest in our humble endeavours, and, under your countenance and patronage, they have prospered. They have prospered so that we have the good fortune to see you amongst us today, surrounded by a large number of those who represent the coming generation of our race. Many of them are representatives of families that have undergone the vicissitudes of time and fortune; but who still retain the remnant of former prestige and social influence in our community. Before many years pass away, they will succeed to the influence which they owe to their descent and the direction which that influence will take cannot be doubted.

The College opened its most elementary classes about six years ago. In 1877, four of its students passed the Entrance Examination of the Calcutta University, five succeeded in 1878, and six in 1879. The College at present educates upto the standard of the First Examination in Arts of the Calcutta University, and the College Committee hopes to begin next year to educate students for the Degree of the Bachelor of Arts of the Calcutta University.

We also take a hopeful view of the pecuniary prospects of our Institution. Besides the money we have collected for the building fund, the College possess an annual income of Rs 21,000, out of which Rs 6,0000 is grant-in-aid we receive from the Government, and the rest is the income from private endowments. This income still falls short of the needs of the College, but the Committee still continues its exertions to increase the resources of the College, and every year sees some additions to it.

This is not an occasion on which it is for us to point out in greater detail the difficulties we have had to contend with, and the manner in which our endeavours have succeeded. We will only say that the progress which the College has made in the past justifies the feelings that our best hopes will be realized some day. We can look forward to the future with confidence; we can feel that as time passes on, the seeds of intellectual activity, which we are sowing, will germinate; that the Muhammadans will cease to be looked upon as the most backward, among British subjects, in the path of civilization and enlightenment. And we flatter ourselves with the hope that the time may not be far distant when the College - the product of our endeavours - may become one of the most powerful centres of education, and one of the greatest agencies for the diffusion of knowledge and civilization amongst our co-religionists.

We, Sir, are proud to feel that, with the success of our endeavours, your name will always be associated. The Central Hall of our College buildings, which is to receive your name, and on the basement of which we are now assembled to greet you, will become some day the scene of the intellectual contests of youthful ambition and educational honours. The annual medal known by your name, will be another means of keeping alive the memory of those obligations to your private good-will and public support to which our success has been mainly due. We shall remember, with sincere gratitude, the honour you have conferred upon us today, by consenting to visit the scene of our labours, and by accepting the Visitorship of our College. And in time to come, when, perhaps, none of us who have received the immediate benefit of your good-will may be alive, your name will still be honoured and gratefully remembered by the future generations, for whose education the Muhammadan Anglo-Oriental College has been founded. They will remember to whose helping hand the establishment of the College has been mainly due; they will inherit from us the feelings which animate us towards you - the feeling of regarding you as our Benefactor and a Patron of the cause of Education and Enlightenment amongst the Muhammadans of India.

Signed on behalf of the Muhammadan Anglo-Oriental College Fund Committee by:

Muhammad Lutf Ali [in Urdu], President
Sayyid Baqir Ali Khan [in Urdu], Vice-President
Syed Ahmed, Secretary

Aligarh
11 December, 1880

22

From: Colonel J.G. Ardagh, C.B.
Private Secretary to the Viceroy

To: Sir Syed Ahmed, K.C.S.I
Honorary Secretary,
M.A.O. College,
Aligarh

Viceregal Lodge,
Simla;

May 21st, 1890

Dear Sir Syed Ahmed,
The report upon the Mahomedan Anglo-Oriental College at Aligarh, together with your explanatory letter, have been laid before the Viceroy, and His Excellency desires me to thank you for making him acquainted with the rules and practical working of the Institution which has long been known to him by repute, as having received the patronage and support of his predecessors.

Your letter gives a concise summary of the origin and development of the College.

Lord Lansdowne observes with satisfaction, that while it is open to students of every creed and race, and while many of the educational staff are Europeans, the religious scruples of the Mahomedan students, both of the Sunni and Shia rites, have been carefully respected, and he trusts that the opposition which the earlier leaders of the movement met with on the part of some of their co-religionists has been to a great extent dissipated, and that the utility of secular education of scientific and literary character is now generally recognised by the whole Mahomedan community in India, as it undoubtedly was by the earlier followers of Islam.

Twelve years have now passed since the School was raised to the status of a College, and nine years since it was affiliated to an University. Numerous endowments and scholarships have been created by the munificence of various well-wishers of the College, and the Viceroy observes with pleasure the liberality of certain great Chiefs who do not profess the Mahomedan religion, but who have, nevertheless, joined in affording material support to the Institution.

The statistics relating to the numbers who have resided in the College, and who have attended the courses of instruction, have not been placed before His Excellency, but from the abstract given in your letter, he observes that but few proceed to take the degree of B.A., only 26 having been successful in nine years. Lord Lansdowne has remarked that in India an University degree appears to be chiefly valued as a stepping stone to employment in the public service; but, while admitting the importance of their particular aim, he observes with some regret, that the upper class do not here, as in other countries regard a liberal education as one of the first duties which they owe to their children; and he is inclined to attribute to this neglect some share at least in the decadence which it is admitted has befallen many of the families which formerly enjoyed considerable influence, and which it is alleged affects the Mahomedan community in particular, as you observe at the commencement of your letter.

The Viceroy hopes that the benefits to be derived from Aligarh College, and other establishments of a like nature, will receive, as time goes on, a wider recognition, and that the pursuit of knowledge will come to be regarded as a thing desirable in itself, and not merely a means to an end.

He remarks that the designation of the College is peculiarly appropriate as connecting that which is English with that which is Mahomedan and Oriental; and he is disposed to lay some stress upon the advantages to be derived from a thorough acquaintance with English as the language of higher culture common to all the subjects of the Queen-Empress throughout her Indian dominions.

In order to give tangible proof of his interest in the College, His Excellency directs me to inform you that it will afford him much pleasure to continue the patronage which was extended to the

Institution by previous Viceroys; and I am to transmit to you as Secretary a donation of five hundred rupees to be applied to such purposes as the Trustees may decide.

Lord Lansdowne has also expressed a wish to have some details as to the curriculum, with a view to encouraging proficiency by the grant of a medal under suitable condition.

I remain,
your faithfully

(Sd) J.C.Ardagh, Colonel,
Private Secretary to the Governor-General.

23

From T.W.Holderness, Esq
Secretary to Govt., N.W.P. & Oudh

To: H.Babington Smith, Esq.,
Private Secretary to Viceroy

Allahabad;
January 9th, 1897

Dear Sir,
The Lieutenant-Governor has asked me, in compliance with the wish expressed in His Excellency the Viceroy's telegram, to send you the following names for the Central Famine Committee to represent these Provinces. His excellency mentioned 15 or 20 names as a limit; but His Honour has found it difficult to represent all interests and portions of the Province in fewer names than the list contains.

The provincial list, which will be formed under the rules, will of course be much larger.

Yours truly

(Sd) T.W. Holderness

[Enclosure to the foregoing letter]

List of Gentlemen nominated by His Honour the Lieutenant-Governor and Chief Commissioner, North-Western Provinces and Oudh, to represent the Provinces on the Central Famine Committee.

North-Western Provinces

His Highness Maharaja Prabhu Narayan Singh Bahadur, K.C.I.E., of Benares

Raja Lal Ram Pratap Singh, of Manda, Allahabad District.

Raja Hari Raj Singh, of Kashipur, Moradabad District.

Raja Satrujit Pratap Bahadur Sahi, of Tamkuhi, Gorakhpur District.

Nawab Mumtazuddaula Muhammad Faiyyaz Ali Khan, of Pahsu, Bulandshahr District.

Raja Fateh Singh, of Pawayan, Shahjahanpur District.

Raja Balwant Singh, of Awa, Etah District

Maulvi Sir Saiyad Ahmad Khan Bahadur, K.C.S.I., of Aligarh

Seth Lachhman Das, C.I.E., of Mutra

24

From: H. Babington Smith, Esq.
Private Secretary to Viceroy
Viceregal Lodge,
Simla

To: Sir Syed Ahmed Khan Bahadur, K.C.S.I
President of the General Committee for the Celebration of the Sixty year's reign of H.M. the Queen Empress of India.

Sir,
As soon as I received your letter of the 1st instant, I laid it before His Excellency the Viceroy, and His Excellency at once took steps to ascertain His majesty's wishes with regard to the deputation which the Mahomedans of India, as represented by your committee, desired to send to England on the occasion of the completion of the sixtieth year of Her Majesty's reign.

My telegram of the 22nd instant has informed you of the directions which Her Majesty has been pleased to give; and I am desired by His Excellency the Viceroy to say, that while he recognises how highly those to whom it was proposed to entrust this duty would have valued the honour of presenting an address to her majesty in person, he has no doubt that al will feel that Her Majesty's wishes are paramount.

The Queen Empress has authorised the Viceroy to receive addresses on her behalf, and, if your Committee should desire to send a deputation to present the address to Viceroy at Simla, His Excellency will be happy to make arrangements for receiving it.

I am desired to say that the other proposal for the celebration which are explained in your letter have His Excellency's cordial approval, and that he has observed with the highest satisfaction this renewed evidence of the loyal devotion of the Mahomedans of India to the Throne of Her Majesty the Queen Empress.

I have the honour to be,

Sir,

Yours most obedient Servant

(Sd) H. Babington Smith
Private Secretary to the Viceroy

25

Telegram, 22nd April 1897, 3-15 p.m.

From: Private Secretary to Viceroy, Simla.

To: Mahomed Hyat Khan, C.S.I.,
Jullundur

The Viceroy has now received a reply from England with regard to the proposed Jubilee Deputation. As you are aware, Her Majesty is away from England, and this has no doubt made it impossible to ascertain her wishes earlier.

I am sending the following telegram to Sir Syed Ahmed Khan:-

Begins: On receipt of your letter of April 1st, detailing the steps proposed by the Mahomedans of India for the celebration of the completion of the sixtieth year of Her Majesty's reign, I at once laid it before the Viceroy, and His Excellency telegraphed to the secretary of State requesting him to present an address to Her Majesty. The reply has now been received, and, in view of the special circumstances of the year, which have involved also departure from the precedent of

1887 in regard to the reception of Chiefs in England, Her Majesty has been pleased to direct that address should on this occasion be submitted through Government, and not personally, and has authorised the Viceroy to receive loyal addresses on her behalf,

A letter follows, replying on the other matters mentioned in your letter. *Ends*

26

Telegram, 22nd April, 1897, 3-15 p.m.
From: Private Secretary to Viceroy,
Simla.

To: Sir Syed Ahmed Khan Bahadur,
Aligarh.

On receipt of your letter of April Ist, detailing the steps proposed by the Mahomedans of India for the celebration of the completion of the sixtieth year of Her Majesty's reign, I at once laid it before the Viceroy, and His Excellency telegraphed to the Secretary of State requesting him to present an address to Her Majesty.

The reply has now been received, and, in view of the special circumstances of the year, which have involved also departure from the precedent of 1887 in regard to the reception of Chiefs in England, Her Majesty has been pleased to direct that address should on this occasion be submitted through Government, and not personally, and has authorised the Viceroy to receive loyal addresses on her behalf.

A letter follows, replying on the other matters mentioned in your letter. *Ends*

27

Telegram, 22nd April 1897, 3.15 p.m.

From: Private Secretary to Viceroy, Simla.

To: Sir Syed Ahmed Khan Bahadur, Aligarh.

On receipt of your letter of April 1st, detailing the steps proposed by the Mahomedans of India for the celebration of the completion of the sixtieth year of Her Majesty's reign, I at once laid it before the Viceroy, and His Excellency telegraphed to the Secretary of State requesting him to take Her pleasure with regard to the proposed deputation to present an address to Her Majesty.

The reply has now been received, and, in view of the special circumstances of the year, which have involved also departure from the precedent of 1887 in regard to the reception of Chiefs in England, Her Majesty has been pleased to direct that addresses should on this occasion be submitted through Government, and not personally, and has authorised the Viceroy to receive loyal addresses on her behalf.

A letter follows, replying on the other matters mentioned in your letter.

28

From: H.Babington Smith, Esq.,
Private Secretary to the Viceroy.

Viceregal Lodge,
Simla;

April 24th, 1897.

To:

Sir Syed Ahmed Khan Bahadur, K.C.S.I
President of the General Committee for the Celebration of the Sixty Year's reign of H.M. the Queen Empress of India.

Sir,
As soon as I received your letter of the Ist instant, I laid it before His Excellency the Viceroy, and His Excellency at once took steps to ascertain Her Majesty's wishes with regard to the deputation which the Mahomedans of India, as represented by your committee, desired to send to England on the occasion of the completion of the sixtieth year of Her Majesty's reign.

My telegram of the 22nd instant has informed you of the directions which Her Majesty has been pleased to give; and I am desired by His Excellency the Viceroy to say, that while he recognises how highly those to whom it was proposed to entrust this duty would have valued the honour of presenting an address to Her Majesty in person, he has no doubt that all will feel that Her Majesty's wishes are paramount.

The Queen Empress has authorised the Viceroy to receive addresses on her behalf, and, if your Committee should desire to send a deputation to present the address to the Viceroy at Simla, His Excellency will be happy to make arrangements for receiving it.

I am desired to say that the other proposals for the celebration of this occasion which are explained in your letter have His Excellency's cordial approval, and that he has observed with the highest satisfaction this renewed evidence of the loyal devotion to the Mahomedans of India to the Throne of Her Majesty the Queen Empress.

I have the honour to be

Sir

Yours most obedient servant

(Sd) H. Babington Smith
Private Secretary to the Viceroy

29

From: His Honour Sir A.P.MacDonnell, K.C.S.I
Lieutenant-Governor of the N.W.P. & Oudh

To: His Excellency The Earl of Elgin & Kincardine, G.M.S. &.c.

Lieut.-Governor's Camp,
N.W.P. & Oudh,
May 9th, 1897

Dear Lord Elgin,
My last letter to your Excellency was written before I started on tour in the Meerut and Rohilkhand Divisions. In the Meerut Division I found things in a satisfactory state. A little relief to a few hundred persons, *purdanasheen* and beggars, was being given in only two places, Aligarh and Saharanpur, the cost being met by local subscriptions. No relief was really necessary; but as the business was being managed by non-official agency, and as it was to come to an end when the rains broke, I do not think it necessary to interfere. No relief from public money, nor from the charitable Relief Fund, is being administered; none is wanted.

At Aligarh Sir Syud Ahmed came to see me, and he spoke at length about the state of Mahomedan feeling. The burden of his complaint was, that the attitude of the England towards Turkey, and the strict enforcement of "segregation" provisions of the Plague Prevention Rules, were alienating the minds of Mussalmans. He had been, I understood, to Delhi to get subscriptions for the Jubilee presentations, and had had but indifferent success. His remarks on the Plague Rules applied, I understood, more to Bombay and Sindh than to these Provinces. He admitted that if segregation was to be enforced at all, it could not be enforced under less oppressive rules than the North-Western Provinces Rules. I told him that the British Government could not admit the fatalistic doctrine which some Mahomedans pressed on us; that the Government could not see the country ravaged by plague, and commerce killed, because some people preferred their women to die rather than be removed from the sphere of contagion. I warned him that the North-Western Provinces Plague Rules, could only be effective, if strictly acted on in the beginning of an epidemic, and that if not loyally acted on, and cases reported, and dealt with according to the rules, they would not suffice to prevent the malady effecting a lodgement. Once a lodgement has been effected, I told him that I should act with no less resolution than General Gatacre in Bombay. The old gentlemen was seriously alarmed, and he solemnly warned me that the business was creating more ill-will against us than anything he had known since the Mutiny. He also told me he did not at all understand why the Amir of Kabul should take to writing about Jehad, and that he thoroughly mistrusted Abdul Rahman. Sir Syud Ahmed still retains all his difficulties. He never once referred to his son Mahmud. The latter is at Lucknow, going from bad to worse through drink. It is a great pity. In the evening I paid the Syud the compliment of returning his call, when our talk was on social topics, public affairs not being referred to. I have just appointed his nephew to the Provincial Service, for which the old man thanked me. I was sorry to hear from him that the numbers in the College are decreasing. He seems confident that the decrease is due to the hard times we are passing through; but I fear the College is in a downward plane: there seems to be no successor to the Syud. He told me he would on another occasion consult me on the whole subject.

I am,
Dear Lord Elgin,
Yours sincerely

(Sd) A.P. MacDonnell

P.S. I will at once attend to your Lordship's suggestion about native titles. There is the difficulty in these Provinces that all the best men have titles, many hereditary.

30

From: The Right Hon'ble Lord George Hamilton, M.P.
Secretary of State for India.

To: His Excellency
The Earl of Elgin and Kincardine,G.M.S.I.,&.c.

India Office
London;
June 4th, 1897

Dear Lord Elgin,
I have to thank you for your letter of the 12th May. Mackenzie's departure, though sudden, seems to me to have occurred at an opportune moment. The information which you have sent me, together with the official returns from Bengal, seems to show that gratious relief has attained quite abnormal proportions. This coupled, with the very large requisitions upon the Relief Fund, does seems to indicate that relief is being distributed on more lenient and liberal terms than prevail elsewhere. I also hear that the Railway authorities have great difficulty in certain districts in obtaining the labour they require. It was inevitable that as the method of relief became more systematised and the people got accustomed to the relief methods, the coolies should flock to and remain at our relief works. I think you may have to consider whether piece-work should not now be universally applied, with the object of gradually screwing it up until its demand is somewhat in access of the task exacted elsewhere.

I quite agree with you that the reports of the famine operations in the smallest Native States are satisfactory reading, and reflect great credit upon the political officers, who were thus able to so effectually spur the authorities under them to a proper discharge of new duties.

I am glad that MacDonnell is taking a little rest. He certainly required it, and it is difficult for any man to retain the even balance of his judgement when so overworked, and for so long a period as Sir Antony has been. The letter you enclosed to me from him is very interesting reading, though I cannot help thinking that Sir Syud Ahmed exaggerates the state of feeling of the Mahomedan Communities in the North-West.

Sandhurst seems to have really stamped out the plague in the towns of his Presidency, and everything seems to be working smoothly and effectively....

We are now in the full swing of preparations for the Jubilee, and it is clear that for a fortnight at least it will be one continuos bustle and turmoil of ceremony upon ceremony. I am very glad that no deputations from India have come with addresses. I am sure they would have been more or less crowded out of the programme, for neither time, nor the Queen's age, will allow Her Majesty to go through more than a certain amount of ceremonial world, and those who had taken the trouble to come this great distance would, in all probability, have returned to India disappointed and annoyed at the comparatively-speaking small amount of attention given to them whilst in England.

Your suggestion for the ceremony to be held in the afternoon of the 22nd June is a good idea. The Queen, I believe, telegraph on that day a message both to the Colonies and India, and I think we could make this message cover the reply to the addresses. I will, however, telegraph further on this point in a few days.

Believe me

Yours very truly,

(Sd) George Hamilton

31

From: His Excellency The Earl of Elgin and Kincardine,G.M.S.I.,&.C.

To: His Honour Sir A.P.MacDonnell, G,C.S.I.,
Lieutenant-Governor of the N,W.P.& Oudh

Viceregal Lodge,
Simla;
November 2nd, 1897

Dear Sir Antony MacDonnell,
You will have observed that I have found it necessary to abandon my tour in Burma.... I have been thinking how to make use of this interval, and it has occurred to me that if you were still at Allahabad I might take advantage of the invitation you gave me and break our journey there, proceeding afterwards to Darjeeling, which we have not yet seen.

There is another visit which it might be possible for me to pay en route i.e., to Sir Syud Ahmed's College at Aligarh. That has been suggested more than once, but I have not been able to accomplish it. I think a visit at this time might perhaps be a good thing?

My rough idea of the arrangements was that I might leave here on the 25th, stop at Aligarh for a few hours on the 26th, arrive at Allahabad early on 27th, and in convenient to you remain till the Monday evening. Please, however, let me know if all this fits in with your plans. I shall make no final arrangements till I hear from you, but perhaps you will kindly telegraph.

I have to acknowledge your letters of 30th October. I am sorry I left out "Oudh" in my telegram, and am obliged to you for inserting it. ....

Yours sincerely

(Sd) Elgin

32

From: His Honour Sir A.P.MacDonnell, G.C.S.I.,
Lieutenant-Governor of the N,W.P.& Oudh

To: His Excellency
The Earl of Elgin and Kincardine,G.M.S.I.,&.c.

Government House,
Allahabad;
November 5th, 1897

Dear Lord Elgin,
It will be a very great pleasure to see your Excellencies here on the 27th. I hope I may expect to see the young ladies also. My wife, I am sure, will much regret being away and unable to receive you; but her visit to England could not be longer postponed.

I shall await the issue of formal notice from Colonel Durrand's Office, before issuing orders for your Excellency's reception at Allyghar. Your visit to the College, which is well worth seeing, will be great event for the old Sayd, who is a very fine character. His son, Sayd Mahmud, is at present staying with him -a wreck of his former self.

I do not understand your Excellency to wish me to meet you at Allyghar; and as your visit to that place will be but brief, I think I should meet your convenience better by receiving you here. But I am, of course, entirely at your command.

I thank you for your kindness in regard to the Investiture, and remain,

Dear Lord Elgin,

Yours sincerely,
(Sd) A.P.MacDonnell

33

Telegram, 9th November 1897, 4-30 p.m. (recd. 7-30 p.m)

From: Sir Syed Ahmed, Trustee and Life Honorary Secretary of the
Mohamedan Anglo-Oriental College,
Aligarh.

To: Private Secretary to Viceroy,
Simla.

I have been honoured by receipt of a telegram from His Honour Sir Antony Patrick MacDonnell, Lieutenant-Governor of the North-Western Provinces and Chief Commissioner of Oudh, from Allahabad, and, in reply thereto, I have telegraphed the following message which, in order to save time, and also the necessity of further explanation, I repeat in this telegram for submission to His Excellency the Viceroy. My telegram to His Honour Sir Antony MacDonnell runs as follows:

Your Honour's welcome telegram, conveying the tiding of His Excellency the Viceroy's desire to honour the Mohamedan Anglo-Oriental College with a visit on the 26th instant between 11 and 12 o'clock noon, reached me last evening, and, in recognition of such an honour, I summoned a consultation meeting of such of the Trustees of the College as could, without delay, be present at such a meeting. Accordingly, the consultation meeting was held, and it was unanimously decided that I, in my capacity as a Trustee and Life Honorary Secretary of the College should send a telegraphic message to your honour thanking you for your welcome message, and intimating that both the day, namely, the 26th instant, as well as the time above mentioned, will suit the Trustees of the College in order to receive the honour of a visit from His Excellency the Viceroy of India, in whom not only the Trustees of the College, but also other Mohamedans and well-wishers of the College see the representative of their Sovereign Her Majesty the Queen of Great Britain and Ireland and also the Empress of India, under the blessing of whose

Ireland and also the Empress of India, under the blessing of whose more than 60 years reign India has prospered more than it even did before or since. In consequence of the last night's consultation meeting of the Trustees this reply has been delayed. I am also telegraphing to the Private Secretary of His Excellency the Viceroy in terms similar to those contained in this telegraphic message to your Honour.

34

Telegram, 10th November 1897, 9 p.m.

From: Private Secretary to Viceroy,
Simla.

To: Sir Syed Ahmed Khan Bahadur, K.C.S.I,
Aligarh.

His Excellency the Viceroy desires me to thank you for your telegram and for the cordial welcome which, as appears from the Resolution you quote, you and the Trustees of the College are prepared to give him. His Excellency looks forward with pleasure to his visit.

35

Telegram, 19th November 1897,
4-55 p.m.

From: Viceroy,
Simla

To: Lieutenant-Governor, N.W.P

I am sorry not to have replied sooner to your letter about Aligarh. I do not think that there is any necessity for your presence there during my visit, which is a very brief one. I understand that an address will be presented, and I should be glad to learn if there are any special points on which you would think it desirable for me to touch in my reply.

36

From: The Hon'ble Sir A.P.MacDonnell, G.C.S.I.,
Lieutenant-Governor of the N.W.P.& Oudh

To: His Excellency
The Earl of Elgin and Kincardine,G.M.S.I.,&.c.

Government House,
Allahabad;
November 20th, 1897

Dear Lord Elgin,
The chief points to bear in mind in connection with the Aligarh College are, I think, that it is the result of purely independent effort on the part of the Mahomedan community, headed by Sir Syed Ahmed; that the funds have been very largely contributed by Mahomedan Native Chiefs; that the main object of the institution is to educate Mahomedans so as to enable them to compete successfully with their fellow subjects under British rule; and that the declared policy of the College has hitherto been loyalty to the British Government.

Owing to over-confidence in a subordinate (a Hindu I think) on the part of Sir Syed Ahmed and his son, Syed Mahmud, most serious deflections occurred in 1895, or about that time. Over a lakh of rupees was misappropriated. When Syed Mahmud went to the Bar again last year, it was the declared or professed object of recouping his loss from his earnings, and so saving his father's name. Syed Mahmud has not fulfilled this object, I believe.

Some reference may be made to recent appointments in these Provinces from which an inference has been drawn that I am unfavourable to Mahomedans generally. I have mentioned this matter in one of my letters to your Excellency, and when approached on the subject by Mr Morrison (who was acting for Mr Beck), I explained matters to him. He then wrote to the newspapers a letter to which I could take no objection. Briefly, my position is that, while we should appoint the best man, to a vacancy irrespective of creed, we should ordinarily not appoint a majority of Mahomedans to services among a population of which the Mahomedans are only as one to seven. My view is that Mahomedans, owing to various causes, historical and social, should not be limited to the proportion suggested by population, in the matter of Government appointments: but that, if they are appointed roughly in the proportion of three to five Hindus they will be treated very liberally.

The subject is one to be avoided, if possible, but if avoidance is not possible, the above remarks may be of use to your Excellency.

The College has been always distinguished for its promotion of physical training, adopting the maxim *sana in corpore sano principle*. It turns our manly fellows, mostly.

I remain

Dear Lord Elgin

Yours sincerely

(Sd) A.P.MacDonnell

37

Telegram, 29th March 1898, 2.30 p.m.

From: Private Secretary to Viceroy,
Calcutta.

To: Saiyyid Mahmood,
Aligarh.

The Viceroy desires me to convey to you the very great regret with which he has heard of the death of your father, a grievous loss not only to his own family and friends, but to those public interests in whose furtherance his energy and remarkable abilities were employed.

Allow me to add an expression of my own sympathy.

38

From: Haji Mahomed Ismail Khan

To: Chief Secretary to the Govt., N.W.P and Oudh

Aligarh;
April 2nd, 1898

Dear Sir,

The sudden and unexpected death of Sir Syud Ahmed has been such a loss to his community as is fraught with far-reaching consequences. It is not fully realised now, but as time passes its magnitude will unveil itself to the Mahomedans. The immediate effect of this calamity has, however, manifested itself in the disturbed condition of the Mahomedan Anglo-Oriental College, as Sir Syud died at a time when the financial condition of the College was very critical, and we could ill spare him. It may be said without risking the charge of pessimism that the condition of the Mahomedan Anglo-Oriental College has become dangerously critical.

The existence of the Mahomedan Anglo-Oriental College wields such an influence over the national life of Mahomedans of Upper India, that its prosperity or decay, or even a vital change in its constitution, is sure to have for good or for bad an effect on the Mahomedans. Therefore at present juncture it requires the special care and attention of its supporters and well-wishers, and among which I may class the Government itself.

But I must acknowledge that it is easier to say that its supporters should direct their attention to the amelioration of its condition than to point out any particular method for attaining the same, and arresting the mismanagement prevalent at present.

After the death of Sir Syud Ahmed, the opinions expressed about the future management of the College are, as was expected they would be, various and conflicting.

In the opinion of some the Government should take upon itself the management of the Mahomedan Anglo-Oriental College, just like the Agra or the Canning College. Others think the Government should ever deal indulgently with this institution, i.e., only keep a watch over the Proceedings of the Trustees, and interfere only when the Trustees commit a glaring mistake or are charged of gross carelessness, and even then, that interference should be meant to rectify the mistake.
Some persons think that the power of the European Staff of the College, so much so that they should be given the powers of the Secretary of the Trustees (sic). Mr Syud Mahmud, the present Secretary, Mahomedan Anglo-Oriental College, has always done that, in so far as he has appointed Mr T. Beck Principal,

Mahomedan Anglo-Oriental College, Registrar of the College. Those who are against this proposal contend that it will be prejudicial to the interest of the Mahomedans as well as the original scheme of the Founder of the College, who wished to have the Education and moral training of the students in the hands of the European Staff, but wanted the government of the College to rest with a body of independent Mahomdean Trustees.

Then there is the question as to who should be the secretary to the Trustees. Here, again, opinions differ very much. Those who support Mr Syud Mahmud do so with the qualification that he should be kept secretary only in name, while the real business should be carried on by another man called Joint Secretary or any such name.

Others wish that Mr Syud Mahmud should be entirely removed from the post of Secretary, and another man appointed instead. But many difficulties lie in the way of appointing, or more properly, electing a new Secretary. There is a party that wants to appoint Maulvie Samiulla Khan, C.M.G., to this post, by making him a trustee, and then electing him as Secretary, in preference to electing one from present number of the Trustees. But as from long time Maulvie Samiulla Khan and Mr Theodore Beck are not on good terms, and as it is admitted on all hands that, owing to his valuable services, the retention of Mr Beck is necessary for the College, the supporters of Maulvie Samiulla want to effect a reconciliation between the two gentlemen.

As regards the secretaryship itself, there are many who want to set limitations to the nearly undefined and unlimited powers of the Secretary, - powers that had been allowed the late Secretary owing to his influence and confidence in him. They want to see the secretary stripped of all power and to make him mere instrument to carry out the wishes of the Trustees.

The above is, in my opinion, a nearly accurate account of the different opinions at present entertained by the trustees and those who take an interest in the Institution.

Believing that it would be desirable to make the Government acquainted with the real state of things, I have ventured to write this letter for the perusal of His Honour the Lieutenant-Governor. I would beg leave to reserve my own opinion about this matter, as I have been unable to arrive up to this time at definite conclusion.

However, should His Honour be pleased to know the details of the case, I can present myself before him at any time His Honour may graciously appoint.

I remain,

Dear sir,
Yours Truly

Haji Md. Ismail Khan

39

From
Theodore Beck, Esq.
Principal, Mahomedan Anglo-Oriental College, Aligarh

To:
H. Babington Smith, Esq., C.S.I
Private Secretary to the Viceroy,
Aligarh
April 2nd, 1898

My Dear Smith,
A meeting of the Board of Management of the Mahomedan Anglo-Oriental College was held on Thursday at which it was decided to attempt to raise a fund of ten lakhs of rupees as a Memorial to Sir Syed Ahmed with the object of taking a step towards accomplishing the desire of his life - that a Mahomedan teaching University on the model of Oxford and Cambridge should be created in Aligarh. A meeting of the Committee appointed to carry out this object was held yesterday in Aligarh, and I was requested, on behalf of the

Committee, to write to you to ask if His Excellency the Viceroy would be willing to preside at a meeting to be held in Simla towards the end of May or in June, and attended by Mahomedans from various parts of India, in connection with the Memorial Fund.

I know that in making such a request we are not asking a usual thing, but a special act of kindness. Nevertheless I feel that our love and reverence for the old Sir Syed may excuse our doing so. No one has done so much as he for the welfare of the people or the stability of the British Government. And I know that nothing would please him so much, if he were alive, as encouragement given to the cause to which he devoted his life. If His Excellency should very kindly consent, the whole Mahomedan nation would feel that the honour he thus paid to the memory of their leader was an honour to them also. It would touch their hearts: of that I am sure.

I do not wish, nor does any one wish, that the Viceroy, should commit himself and the Government in any way to an expression of opinion that the sum we wish to raise is adequate to the purpose we have in view. The Government could never recognise an institution as having risen to that rank until it had worked for years under its full organisation and given proof of adequate results. But it would be a step in that direction, and the final realisation of the idea might take place long after we are dead or gone. And meanwhile it would place the College on an absolutely firm financial footing, which it very much needs, and would guarantee its stability. I spoke about the matter only a month or two ago to Sir Syed - about the plan of raising ten lakhs with this ultimate object - and he warmly approved. Our object was very warmly and eloquently praised by Sir Antony MacDonnell when he visited the College as Lieutenant-Governor. He said " It is not too much to hope that this College will grow into the Mahomedan University of the future; that this place will become the Cudwa of the East; and that in these cloisters Mahomedan genius will discover, and, under the protection of the British Crown, work out that social, religious, and political regeneration of which neither Mecca nor Istamboul offers a prospect",

I may add that Rs 4,100 have already been promised.

If the Viceroy consents, and we can publish the matter soon, we can arrange for delegates of the various branch committees to come to Simla.

I will only add that if the Government ever wish to do a good turn to this College, and to recognise the efforts which Sir Syed and all of us have made to turn out loyal citizens - this is the time, a time which will perhaps never occur again.

Believe me
ever yours sincerely

(Sd) Theodore Beck.

40

From: H.Babington Smith, Esq., C.S.I
Private Secretary to the Viceroy.

To:
Theodore Beck, Esq.,
Principal, Mahomedan Anglo-Oriental College, Aligarh

Viceroy's Camp.
April 9th, 1898

My Dear Beck,

The Viceroy has read your letter about the proposed to raise a Memorial to Sir Syed Ahmed with great interest, and with every wish for the success of the movement. He has some doubts, however, as to the particular manner in which you suggest that he should associate himself with it. Especially, he is very doubtful whether Simla is the right place for a representative meeting of Mahomedans.

This, however, is not a reply to your request, but merely a warning that you may not go ahead in the meantime with preparations for a meeting of the kind described in your letter. His Excellency would like to think over the matter, and is asking Sir Antony MacDonnell for his opinion.

As soon as we reach Simla (0n the 25th instant) I hope to let you know for certain.

Yours sincerely,

(Sd) H.Babington Smith.

41

From:

His Excellency
The Earl of Elgin and Kincardine, G.M.S.I., etc.

To:

The Hon'ble Sir A.P.MacDonnell,G.C.S.I
Lieutenant-Governor of the N.W.P. & Oudh

Viceroy's Camp;
April 9th, 1898

Dear Sir Antony MacDonnell,
Would you kindly give me your opinion on the proposal contained in the enclosed letter?. You encouraged me to visit the College last year, and I believe you entertained the opinion that Sir Syed's influence with his co-religionists was a good one. Several previous Viceroys have also praised the College and Sir Syed's work in connection with it.

I should not, therefore, like to fall short in anything that was fairly due for me, either in the way of commemorating the Founder, or giving more permanency to the College. But I cannot say that Mr Beck's plan commends itself to me. In the first place, I think the Mahomedans are quite strong enough to make this effort themselves, and that if they are in earnest they ought to do so; and, in the second place, a meeting of the kind at Simla would be very unsuitable. I ought to be held at one of your great Mahomedan centres in the North-Western Provinces, or perhaps at Delhi; and, if it is desirable to appeal to the public outside, I should be better pleased to show my sympathy in the movement by a subscription than by presiding at a meeting where I should, I conceive, be quite out of place.

In the meantime Babington Smith is telling Mr Beck that I have my doubts, and that he had better not make any arrangements till he hears again after my arrival at Simla. This will give me an opportunity of knowing your views.

Yours sincerely

(Sd) Elgin

[Enclosure to the above letter]

Copy of letter from Mr Theodore Beck to Private Secretary to Viceroy, dated 2nd April 1898.

42

From:

The Hon'ble Sir A.P.MacDonnell, G.C.S.I.,
Lieutenant-Governor of the N.W.P.& Oudh

To:

His Excellency,
The Earl of Elgin and Kincardine,G.M.S.I.,&.c.
N.W.P & Oudh;
April 19th, 1898

Dear Lord Elgin,
I have received your letter of April 9th, which encloses copy of letter from Mr Beck of the Aligarh College to Mr Babington Smith. I think that the following remarks on the condition of the Aligarh College will confirm your Excellency in the view that it would be very undesirable for you to what Mr Beck asks, or to commit yourself to any particular course, at present, in regard to the College.

The constitution of the Aligarh College places the power of control in the hands of Trustees, of whom there are 66. Of these Trustees only 35 are resident in the North-Western Provinces and Oudh, and most of these 35 have, I understand, exercised but little active interference in the affairs of the College. The executive work of the Trustees devolves on the managing Committee, which now consists of 14 Members of the College Staff, the 14th being a Hindu gentleman (the College not professing to be, though in practice it substantially is, a purely Mahomedan Institution. The Honorary Secretary and Principal of the College from two out of the six Trustees above mentioned. But though this Board of Management nominally controls the College, the real control rests with the Secretary and Principal; and doubtless with the view to stereotype this concentration of control, it has been recently decided by the Trustees, at the suggestion, I believe, of the late Sir Syud Ahmed, that no Trustee shall be appointed to fill a vacancy in the Board of Management unless nominated to a vacancy by the Honorary Secretary.

The Mahomedans interested in the Institution are divided into two parties. One party, headed by Sir Syud Ahmed, was (and is) in favour of education on English lines, and of liberal principles in religion. The other party is headed by Maulvie Samiulla Khan, C.M.G, late a Subordinate Judge in the Provinces (and a protégé of Sir Auckland Colvin's who took him to Egypt with him when the Maulvie got his C.M.G.). Maulvie Samiulla Khan is not a Trustee; is, or professes to be, an orthodox Mahomedan, and is not in favour of the Liberal policy of Sir Syud. So long as Syud Ahmed lived no one could, with success, question his direction or control. Even when, some three years to go, the Syud's failing health and increasing age reduced his capacity for work, whereby a subordinate was able to embezzle over a lakh of rupees, no one called his dictatorship in question. But it was foreseen that on Sir Syed Ahmud's death a powerful attack would be made with the object of depriving his party of the control of the College: and doubtless, it was with a view of repelling such an attack, that the control of the Secretary and Principal over the Board of Management to which I have referred above was secured.

After Sir Syud Ahmed's death, Syud Mahmud, his son, who was Joint Secretary, became Secretary under Article 44 of the College Regulations; while under article 46, the Secretary, instead of calling on the Trustees to appoint a Joint Secretary, has appointed Mr Beck as Registrar of the College with function of a Secretary. It has thus come to pass that the whole management of the College has come into the hands of Syud Mahmud and Mr Beck, while as the former is, as your Excellency knows, unfortunately not always able to transact business, the management must mainly devolve on Mr Beck. My belief is that this state of things will not be long tolerated by the body of intelligent Mahomedans interested in the College, nor indeed do I think it conducive to the welfare of that Institution.

If your Excellency were, in the present state of affairs, to acquiesce in Mr Beck's request, your position might be misunderstood; and many might believe that you had decided to support Mr Beck and Syud Mahmud against all others.

A few days ago I received from Syud Mahmud a letter, from which I send a copy of the relevant portion. I also received a letter (copy enclosed) from Hadji Mahomed Ishmail Khan, formerly a Member of Lieutenant-Governor's Legislative Council, a Trustee of the College, and the most respectable local member, perhaps, of Syud Ahmed's party. From these two letters you will perceive how troubled the College "politics" are, and how necessary it is that the Government should be very careful in steps or action it takes. The failure of the Aligarh College would be, for these provinces, and indeed for all Mahomedan India, a disaster of great magnitude; and while I shall be prepared, when the situation is developed and the issues are defined, to take, in communication with you or the Government of India, the steps which may seem suitable for maintaining the College on the principles of its founder, it is clear that the time for such action last not yet arrived.

The College Budget for last year shows as expenditure of Rs 76,784 and an income of Rs 75,506. The receipt side of the account, however, contains many substantial items which cannot be regarded as stable; and I am far from satisfied that the financial position of the College is safe. You will observe that Hadji Mahomed Ishmail Khan's words on this matter are very disquieting. The desire of Syud Mahmud and Mr Beck to start a subscription on a large scale, is doubtless prompted as much by the financial situation of the College, as by the laudable desire to perpetuate Sir Syud Ahmed's memory. This Government contributes annually to the College and attached school between 15,000 and 16,000 rupees from our Educational Budget, and I possess, under the constitution of the College, the right to have at any time an audit of the accounts, and an ascertainment of the Institution's financial position. It will probably be necessary that whatever arrangement may be come to between the parties interested in the College, such an ascertainment or verification of the financial condition of the College should be effected before Government undertakes any further responsibility than that which it now incurs. I am thinking that it may be well if, before I go on leave, I invite Syud Mahmud, Mr Beck, and one or two more of the chief Mahomedan Trustees to meet me, and, without prejudice, discuss the situation. Mr La Touche would assist, and would be in position to tender to your Excellency further advice or information on the subject, pending my return.

I am

Dear Lord Elgin

Yours sincerely

A.P.MacDonnell

P.S. I have opened this letter to tell your Excellency that I have decided to invite Mr Mahmud and Mr Beck to see me about the College affairs, either here before the 4th or at Allahabad on the 5th of May. I will let you know the result. The meeting will be merely with the object of ascertaining the position. I do not intend to decide on any action; but I will leave my suggestion with Mr La Touche.

[Enclosures to the above letter]

43

Extract from letter from Mr Syud Mahmud, Life Honorary Secretary of the Mahomedan Anglo-Oriental College, Aligarh, No 146, dated 4th April 1898, to the Private Secretary to His Honour the Lieutenant-Governor, North-Western Provinces.

Para.4. Since His Honour the Lieutenant-Governor honoured the College with his visit not long ago, it may possibly interest him to know that under the College Laws and Regulations which were originally passed in 1889, and which have repeatedly been confirmed by the Trustees of the College, the last occasion being so recent as their Annual Meeting held on the 30th January last (1898), I have by reason of the law succeeded my father in the responsible office of Life Honorary Secretary of the College, and that is the capacity I have taken over charge of all the affairs of the College, and, in consultation with some of the most prominent Trustees of the College as well as Mr Theodore Beck, Principal of the College, made arrangements for the carrying on the work of the College, and for safety of its records and property, etc. and that as soon as practicable, I am going to submit a report upon the affairs of the College to the Government which, under the laws of the College, holds the position of being its patron, and as such entitled and empowered to exercise a supervisionary control upon the College affairs. I may also be permitted to add the expression of hope that the present arrangements as to the constitution and Government of the

College and the excellence of the European and Native Staff of the Collage furnish every expectation that it will continue to hold the important educational status and position which it now holds in India, and that it may in future prosper more than it has done.

Para 5. I have, in the meantime, in consultation with some of the most prominent and earnest trustees of the College, as well as Mr Principal Theodore Beck and some other Members of the European Staff of the College, made provisional arrangements to secure the constitution and the working of the College from the attacks of some of its enemies of long standing who, in consequence of opposing and working against the original aims and ends which my lamented father had in view in founding the College, were expelled by the Trustees in their formal Meetings and Proceedings from having any concern whatsoever with the affairs of an Institution such as the Mahomedan Anglo-Oriental College with which they, by their words of mouth, oral and written, have, for some years past, proved themselves to have no sympathy, and who by their action have no doubt that they wish to employ the vulgar element of bigotry and affected orthodoxy to disturb the peaceful working of the College by the combined efforts and full accord of feeling between Mahomedan Trustees and Mr Principal Theodore Beck and other Members of the European Staff of the College.

6. These matters will be fully explained in the Official Report which it is my duty in my capacity as Life Honorary Secretary of the College to submit to Government as soon as practicable, for I have for the last five months or so been living at Aligarh, giving up my professional practice as a Barrister at Lucknow, in order to master the details connected with this matter, and I do not intend to leave Aligarh till matters regarding the College affairs are placed upon a firmer footing than its enemies are inclined to suppose.

Trusting that you will be good enough to submit this letter to His Honour the Lieutenant-Governor of the North-Western Provinces and Oudh.

44

To;

The Hon'ble Sir A.P.MacDonnell, G.C.S.I.,
Lieutenant-Governor of the N.W.P.&
Oudh

From: His Excellency,
The Earl of Elgin and
Kincardine,G.M.S.I.,&.c.

Viceroy's Camp,
Narkanda;
April 22nd, 1898

Dear Sir Antony MacDonnell,
Many thanks for your letter of the 19th about Aligarh College. I will wait to hear the result of the meeting you have arranged before I do or say anything more.

I am exceedingly loath to suggest anything that might interfere with the completeness of your holiday, but I venture to mention one matter in which I think you could be of the greatest service to us while in England. You are no doubt aware of the general tenor of the policy in regard to currency which we have proposed to the Secretary of State..........

We have been having a capital march through the hills, and I feel I ought now to be quite fit for my few remaining months of work.

Yours sincerely
(Sd) Elgin

45

From:

The Hon'ble Sir A.P.MacDonnell, G.C.S.I.,
Lieutenant-Governor of the N.W.P.& Oudh

To: His Excellency
The Earl of Elgin and Kincardine,G.M.S.I.,&.c.

Allahabad;
[May?] 5th, 1898

Dear Lord Elgin,
I had an interview to-day with Syud Mahmud and Mr Beck. They produced certain accounts; but on going through them with them I saw that they could not be accepted as a substantially complete or accurate statement of the position of the College from the financial point of view - not that I think there is any intention to conceal matters, but simply that the accounts are in great confusion. Sir Syud Ahmed seems to have kept them very much in his own hand; and now that he is gone they have to be disentangled by people previously unconnected with them. I think that the first thing to be done is to have an audit by the Government and a full ascertainment of the financial position of the College. The Government is entitled to do this by the Regulations of the College; and as we accepted the Regulations, a responsibility attaches to us to have the audit in existing circumstances made. It is clear that mistrust at present attaches to the finances, and the audit will do much to clear that off, or to let us know how far assistance is needed. Syud Mahmud and Mr Beck accepted with gratitude my suggestion that an audit should be made, and I am writing to Mr La Touche on the subject. The College is paying the Bank of Bengal Rs.300 per mensem interest on overdrafts, and no money is coming in from subscriptions. The various meetings which have been held have only brought in promises for about Rs.12,000 (out of Mr Beck's estimate of ten lakhs)

I understand that at the general meeting of Trustees to take place either in June or December next the present management will be challenged, but I could not gather what chance of success that attack has. Probably things will :slide" and if some help from Government is not forthcoming the Institution will fall. That would be a pity.

I think that it would not be well for your Excellency to preside at the proposed public meeting; but if you could see your way to express your sympathy with the maintenance of the College as an Educational institution, it would do the institution good.

Syud Mahmud told me as a fact that Mahomedan Maulvies had preached in their mosques that we had invented the plague in order to enable our police, &c, to enter people's houses and rob them, that Government might thus recoup itself for the cost of the Afghan War. To my objection that people whom we had lavished *crores* in saving from famine would believe us to be so base, he said that he had also heard it stated that we saved the people from famine just as ryot saves his bullock from cart, that the bullock might drag the plough, and thus put money in the ryot's pocket!

I don't say this as deserving of general credence, but as a sample of what the evil-disposed say, and the difficulties under which we labour in this country. The Mahomedans are far more bitter against us than the Hindus I believe.

I now bid tour Excellency good-by, and with every possible good wish for your and Lady Elgin's continued good health and happiness.

I am,

My Lord

Yours sincerely,

(Sd) A.P.MacDonnell.

46

From: His Excellency
The Earl of Elgin and Kincardine, G.M.S.I., etc.

To:
The Hon'ble Mr J.J.D.La Touche, C.S.I
Offg. Lieut.Governor of the N.W.P. and Oudh

Viceregal Lodge
Simla,
May 9th, 1898.

My Dear La Touche,
I do not know that it is necessary to do so, but I write a few lines to express the hope that during your tenure of the Lieutenant-Governorship you will not fail to use the utmost freedom in writing to me if any occasion should arise on which you would prefer to communicate with me direct. I value extremely this free intercourse with the Heads of the Local Administrations.

I had a letter from Sir A.MacDonnell in which he referred to several matters which he had handed over to you - Plague Regulations, the Aligarh College, etc. The first course is by far the most important, and we are anxious to see the proposed revision of the Regulations for the North-Western Provinces before we proceed with a general consideration of the subject.

I was sorry to hear that you had been unwell, but hope you are again fully fit for work.

Yours sincerely

(Sd) Elgin

47

From:

The Hon'ble Mr J.D.La Touche,C.S.I.

To:

His Excellency
The Earl of Elgin and Kincardine,G.M.S.I &c.

Lieutenant-Governor's Camp,
N.W.P and Oudh.
May 12th, 1898

My Dear Lord Elgin,
I received last evening your Excellency's letter of 9th May. I had written in the morning a short letter announcing the fact that I had assumed charge. I value greatly the privilege accorded to me of communicating freely and unreservedly with your Excellency, either directly or through your Private Secretary, and I shall not fail to avail myself of it. I thought, however, that I should wait a little before writing on general subjects.

The file of the plague arrangements was the first I called for. I had accompanied Sir Antony MacDonnel to Hardwar on 31 March, after I had left Calcutta, and he had fully explained to me his views before making overcharge. It was only three days ago that I was able to obtain a proof of the Revised Regulations which were being pushed through the Press. They were finally printed yesterday, and a copy goes by to-day's mail to the Home Department and to your Private secretary. The Regulations have been edited with notes by Mr Impey, Secretary in the Judicial Department, and copies are being distributed to all commissioners and collectors.

Sir Antony read to me the correspondence about the Aligarh College. He wrote to me from Allahabad on the importance of obtaining a proper audit of the accounts, so as to show exactly the financial position of the College. This is being arranged for with the

Accountant-General. I do not myself that the College will thrive so long as Mr Syud Mahmud is Secretary. The orthodox Muhammadans were willing to condone what they considered the latitudinarianism of Sir Syud Ahmad, but they will not accept his son. Probably also Mr Beck would do well to efface himself somewhat more than he does. Moulvi Samiullah Khan a few days ago wrote proposing to come up to see me. He is practically the head of the orthodox or reactionary party. I shall see him and learn what he says and inform your Excellency. I believe he can command considerable support from the Muhamnmadan land-owners of Aligarh.

A question on which the Government of India will soon be addressed is that of the civil staff...........

I had a very nasty attack of influenza in Calcutta, but I got right when I reached the dry heat of the North-Western Provinces, and am now quite fit for work.

Yours sincerely

(Sd) J.D.La Touche

48

From:

The Hon'ble Mr J.J.D.LaTaouche, C.S.I.,
Offg. Lieut.-Governor of the N.W.P. & Oudh

To:

H.Babington Smith, Esq., C.S.I
Private Secretary to the Viceroy.

Government House,
Naini Tal;
May 25th, 1898

My Dear Smith,
I enclose, for the information of His Excellency, a Note on the affairs of the Aligarh College. Its accounts and financial position will be subjected to professional audit and examination at the end of June, but I do not anticipate that the results will differ much from the conclusions in my Note. It is important, however, that the financial position should be clearly ascertained and published.

I shall visit the plains early in July, and if invited by the Memorial Fund Committee, will meet them at Aligarh. It is desirable to give them an opportunity of explaining publicly what they are doing and what are their aims.

My theme will be the need for self-help and self-reliance, the necessity for clearing off the debt, the importance of proper arrangements for the security of Endowment Fund, and the abandonment of too ambitious aims.

Yours sincerely

(Sd) J.D. La-Touche

[Enclosure to the foregoing letter]

Note on the Muhammadan Anglo-Oriental College, Aligarh.

I have now had an opportunity of discussing the affairs of the Aligarh College with several gentlemen interested in the welfare of the College, and especially with Mr Beck, Haji Ismail Khan, and Maulavi Sami-ullah Khan.

It is admitted on all sides that the presence of Mr Mahmud as Life Secretary of the College is an immense difficulty. He is invested with the plenary powers conferred by the rules on his father and (rule 122) is the only person entitled to draw cheques. Haji Ismail Khan and Sami-ullah Khan both urge that as long as Mr Mahmud is Secretary the College can not thrive.

The Muhammadans, they say, have lost confidence in him. Having regard to the moral and religious training of their sons they will not send them to a College managed by Mr Mahmud nor will they subscribe money if he is to spend it.

It is practically impossible, however, to get rid of Mr Mahmud. He will not resign, and as he holds office in accordance with a Regulation of the College, he can only be replaced (rule 117) by a two-third majority of the Trustees at their annual meeting in December or January. But it is not likely that such a majority of the Trustees would agree to repeal the Regulation.

Mr Beck has spoken to many of them. The general view is that Mr Mahmud has done much for the College in n former days, and that possibly he may amend, and, in any case, should not be rejected without a longer trial. He is not likely to live long if he continues the present habits. Moreover, it would be very prejudicial to the welfare of the College if public attention were diverted to this question, and if the matter became the subject of dispute among the Trustees. All should join together in the endeavour to establish the College on a secure basis.

The immediate problem before the friends of the College is therefore how to provide, while Mr Mahmud remains Secretary, for the satisfactory management of the Institution. It is necessary to give the public confidence in the financial administration and to make it impossible for any Secretary to spend the money unwisely. It is necessary to arrange so that the Muhammadans should feel that the College is being worked by Muhammadans, and that affairs are not allowed to drift nor committed to the sole management of a European.

Mr Mahmud has in the exercise of the power conferred on him by Rule 46, appointed Mr Beck Registrar of the College. As Registrar Mr Beck has large legal powers, but he fully recognises the need that he should keep in the background and work through Committees of Muhammadans. The business which Sir Syed used to keep in his own hands has been sub-divided. A strong finance Committee has been appointed with Nawab Mohsin-ul-Mulk as President. The task of collecting subscriptions has been made over to the Syed Ahmad Memorial Fund Committee. Building has been stopped except a little that Maulvi Zain-ul-Abidin is carrying out at his own expenses. The business of the Book Shop and of the Conference has been entrusted to Muhammadans. The ordinary routine work of accounts is all that Mr Beck keeps in his own hands. Mr Mahmud has written to the Bank of Bengal, Agra, directing that no cheques shall be paid except on the countersignature of the Registrar. He could cancel this order at any moment, but is not likely to do so. The Finance Committee have passed a Resolution that the accounts shall be audited every year by a professional auditor. There is a general desire that the Finance Committee should be enacted into a Regulation. The result of this distribution of Sir Syed Ahmad's work is that a large number of energetic Muhammadans are taking an active part in the management of the College, a thing which they never had a chance of doing while Sir Syed Ahmad was alive. Mr Beck's services are looked on a indispensable even by those whom he considers antagonistic, and Mr Beck has, I think, succeeded to a large extent in enlisting the energy and public spirit of past students in helping in the management and getting things into order. This is encouraging and of good presage for the future.

Should Mr Mahmud resign, or the post of Secretary become vacant, there are four possible candidates. The best would be Nawab Mohsin-ul-Mulk, but he has bad health, and would not undertake the duties if other suitable men could be found.

The Muhammadans of Aligarh District and City would prefer Samiullah Khan, and are ready to support him. He cannot, however, now be appointed as he is not a Trustee, and it is doubtful if he would obtain a majority of votes among the Trustees. Many dislike him as he came openly came forward to oppose Sir Syed Ahmad Khan in the Public Press. Of his ability there is no doubt, but he is not trusted. The other two possible Secretaries are Mushtak Husen of Amroha, and Haji Ismail Khan. The first is of the bigoted type of Muhammadan. The second is probably the least able of the four.

The College is in debt to the amount of Rs.60,000. About half of this consists of debentures which can be paid off when the Collage becomes more prosperous. The amount due for current debt is Rs.7,000, and there is an overdraft of Rs.18,000. The total debt which now should be paid are Rs 25,000. This debt is the result of the embezzlement of a lakh of rupees in Sir Syed Ahmad's life time. In those days there were no systematized accounts, and it seems probable that rent and tuition fees, which were not as a matter of fact realized, were shown as paid by credit of donations received by Sir Syed Ahmad for the support of the College.

Sir Antony MacDonnell, before he left India, had an interview at Allahabad with Mr Mahmud and Mr Beck about the affairs of the College. They both welcomed the suggestion that the first thing to be done was to have an audit and ascertainment of the precise financial position of the Collage. The College is now closed for the summer vacation, but it will reopen on 25th June, and arrangements have been made with the Accountant-General to carry out an audit extending not only to an examination of the College books, but also to an ascertainment of the permanent source of income. The audit will be made in the first days of July.

Meanwhile Mr Beck has given me the enclosed paper which shows very approximately the expenditure and income of the College. The normal expenditure is Rs.75,000 and exceeds the annual income by Rs.10,000 a year. Certain economies have been achieved amounting to about Rs.250 a month, and at present the College is working with one Professor short, and saving his pay, Rs 400 a month. At present the income nearly equals the expenditure, but there is no margin whatever.

Mr Beck is of opinion that to work the College properly with a competent Staff of Professors, especially adding Professors of History and Philosophy, and to provide for the reasonable development of the College, an income of a lakh a year is necessary.

The Syed Ahmad Memorial Fund Committee are now endeavouring to raise funds amounting to 10 lakhs in order to establish a teaching University. The whole idea is crude and premature. If the Committee succeeds in collecting ten lakhs, the interest on this at 3 1/2 percent would be Rs.325,000, and this, added to the present income of Rs 65,000, would only amount to a lakh: not more than sufficient to maintain a first-class College. It would have been much better if nothing had been said about an University. Mr Beck's real aim is to improve the College that ultimately (perhaps after two generations) it may be in a position to fix its own course of study. The notion of a teaching University, as understood by Mr Beck, is quite strange in India.

A short time ago I received an official application for permission for the Collector of Aligarh to become Treasurer of the Memorial Fund. This I refused on several grounds, and because the money so paid in would be at the disposal of the Secretary who could direct payment to be made as he pleased.

The Memorial Fund Committee are now, I understand, arranging to pay in subscriptions to their own credit to the Bank of Bengal. The Committee includes all Trustees willing to join; all Members of the Board of Management and some old students of the College. They have powers to add to their numbers. They are, however, a body distinct from the governing body of the College, and at present it is desirable that they should remain distinct.

I think it would be a help to the College if I visited Aligarh in July and asked the Memorial Fund Committee to meet me. It would be a good opportunity for them to place the Fund on a basis which would be permanent. The present arrangement do not command the confidence of the public. I do not think that the Memorial Fund should be devoted to wiping out debt. It should be a permanent endowment. The capital should be deposited in the Bank of Bengal and from time to time be invested in Trust Securities with the consent of a competent Board of Directors of the Fund.

The interest only should be handed over to the Trustees for the purpose of strengthening and importing the College. The transfer of capital to the College should be made a difficult proceeding, and possibly there would be no objection to the sanction of the Local Government being obtained before transfer.

A separate subscription should be raised to liquidate the debt of Rs.25,000. There are many of Sir Syed Ahmad's friends who would like to see this debt removed, especially as the debt was caused by the embezzlement of money a few years ago, and it is well known that that embezzlement was a source of permanent grief to Sir Syed Ahmad.

24 May, 1898
Naini Tal

(Sd) J.D. La Touche.

Monthly Source of Income

Particular	Amount Rs As P	Remarks
Government Grant-in-aid.	1,300-0-0	
Municipal aid.	100-0-0	
Jagir endowed by H.H. the Nizam of Hyderabad.	1,980-0-0	
Jagir granted by Salar Jang	94-0-0	
Yaumia Dawani of Rampur State.	100-0-0	
Yaumia Dawani of Patiala State.	150-0-0	
Raza Hosein Endowments.	24-8-5 1/2	
Yaumia Dawani of H.H. the Maharaja of Vizianagram.	-------	
Nizamia Scholarships-Interest on Government.	---------	
Promissory Notes for Wazifas, scholarships of the value of Rs.30,800.	232-0-0	
Fixed deposit of H. Abdul Karim of Rs 5,000 at 6 per cent.	25-0-0	
Fixed deposit for the		

scholarship in the Allahabad Bank at 4 per cent of Rs. 4,300	14-0-0
Interest of 5 shares of Couper Mill Co.Lucknow. Rs 500.	4-0-0
House rent of Bungalows.	300-0-0
House rent, Boarding House, etc.	872-0-0
Tutional fee, School, Day Scholars.	155-0-0
Tutional fee, College, Day Scholars.	72-4-0
Law Class fees	56-8-0
Total Rs.	5379*-4-5 1/2

[*Sic. The items as stated make a total of Rs. 5,479-4-5 1/2]

Monthly Expenses

Particulars	Amount Rs As P	Remarks
College Staff	3,545-0-0	
School Staff	1,338-0-0	
Secretary's expenses:-		
1. Staff	179-0-0	
2. Office Printing	75-0-0	
3. Office	75-0-0	
	329-0-0	
College printing	12-0-0	
Travelling expenses	20-0-0	
College furniture	10-0-0	
Chaukidars	33-0-0	
Mosque servants	27-0-0	
Sundries	50-0-0	
Repairs	130-0-0	
Garden	20-0-0	
Debenture interest	120-0-0	

Overdraft Interest	180-0-0
Institute	200-0-0
Pay of Nasir Khan	15-0-0
Prizes, Medals, & c.	23-0-0
Medical charges	165-0-0
Auditor's fee	40-0-0
Yearly Total Rs. 6,257-0-0	**75,084**

49

To: The Hon'ble Mr J.D.La Touche, C.S.I.
Offg. Lieutenant-Governor of the N.W.P and Oudh

From:
His Excellency The Earl of Elgin and Kincardine, G.M.S.I &c.

Viceregal Lodge
Simla.
June 15th, 1898

Dear Mr La Touche,
I received your letter of the 11th as Hewett was coming up to see me, and I at once spoke to him about the Plague Regulations.

I have asked Babington Smith to write to you about the Aligarh College, because he has seen Mr Beck. I am deferring any interview with him till I have your advice on the line I should assume.

Yours sincerely

(Sd) Elgin

50

To:

The Hon'ble Mr J.J.D.La Touche, C.S.I
Offg.Lieut.Governor of the N.W.P. and Oudh

From:

H.Babington Smith, Esq., C.S.I
Private Secretary to the Viceroy

Viceregal Lodge,
Simla;
June 15th, 1898

Dear Mr La Touche,
The Viceroy desires me to thank you for your note on the affairs of the Mahomedan Anglo-Oriental College, Aligarh, which you forwarded to me with your letter of the 25th May.

Since receiving your letter I have had a long conversation with Mr Beck who is at present in Simla, on the affairs of the College, and have reported what he said to the Viceroy.

His excellency now desires me to explain to you how he regards the present position of affairs, and to ask your advice on certain points with regard to the future. In the first place he gathers that you agree with Sir Antony MacDonnell that " the failure of the Aligarh College would be for this Province and indeed for all Mahomedans India a disaster of great magnitude", and that you think it desirable that, when the suitable time has come, official encouragement for assistance should be to the College in order to supplement the efforts which the governing body may themselves make to establish the position of the College on a more satisfactory basis; but that you think that until the audit has been carried out and the financial position of the College made clear, the time for such action has not yet come. His Excellency is inclined to agree in this view generally ; but it appears from the information I have received from Mr Beck that the College is in considerable straits with regard to meeting its immediate liabilities, and that in the case of assistance from the Government it would be emphatically a case of *bis dat qui cito dat.*

The difficulties of the College are of two kinds: first with regard to its internal management; secondly with regard to finance.

1st.- As regards management His Excellency is inclined to think that it would be misfortune if the orthodox and bigoted party were to gain control over curriculum and management of the establishment. There would be considerable danger in this case that the enlightened and successful lines on which the College hitherto been conducted might not be allowed. Moreover Maulvi Samiulla Khan, who appears to be the head of the opposition part (but who, it is to be noted, is not a Trustee of the College) is not a man whose record inspires much confidence or who would be likely to command the respect and support of Mahomedans generally. On the whole, the question of the Constitution seems to be one which can best be fought out by those immediately concerned, subject possibly in the end to approval by Government.

The difficulty which you mention about Syed Mahmud is very serious one. If matters should come to a dead-lock Mr Beck is preparing to bring his influence to bear with him to resign, but he is naturally reluctant to do this, and his view is that matters had better be allowed to remain as they are until some crisis arises. There may also be some advantage in maintaining the present position in this respect until the work of the Finance and other Committees has shown more capacities of the various possible candidates and of the manner in which the business of the College can be most conveniently conducted.

2nd.- There remains the question of finance. Strenuous efforts are being made to raise a Memorial Fund, but at present, owing no doubt in part to the obstacles which you mention, they are not meeting with much success. Mr Beck is very anxious that the continence and favour of the Government should be expressed in some unmistakable form, and no doubt if this were done it might be of material assistance to him in raising subscriptions. One way of doing this will be if the Viceroy were himself to make a contribution to the Fund, and were to write at the same time a letter expressing his approbation of the objects aimed at by the College, and urging the importance of financial support to so useful an Institution. If, as you suppose, you visit Aligarh in July, and meet the Memorial Fund Committee, it appears to His Excellency that that would be an excellent opportunity for making public such a declaration, and perhaps the most convenient way would be if a letter such as I have described were sent to you for the purpose of being read at the meeting. But in the first place His Excellency would be glad to have your opinion of this suggestion.

The second way in which the Government might assist the finances of the College would be by a substantial contribution, either in the form of a lump sum or in the form of an increase to the monthly grant. Any such contribution would, I suppose, have to come from the Educational Budget of the North-Western Provinces, and His Excellency would at present only suggest for your consideration whether, in view of the importance of maintaining the College in activity and efficiency, it might not be desirable to help them in this way.

Yours sincerely
(Sd) H.Babington Smith.

51

From: The Hon'ble Mr J.J.D.La Touche, C.S.I
Offg. Lieutenant Governor of the N.W.P. and Oudh

To: H.Babington Smith, Esq., C.S.I
Private Secretary to the Viceroy

Naini Tal
June 20th, 1898

My Dear Smith,
I reply to your letter of 15th June. I entirely agree with Sir Antony MacDonnell that the failure of Aligarh College would be for this Province and indeed for all Muhammadan India, a disaster of great magnitude.

Sir Syed Ahmad has succeeded in establishing a College, the aim of which is not merely instruction, but the formation of character, the encouragement of many pursuits, and the promotion of a feeling of self-respect among the students. If the College were to fail, Muhammadan students could obtain instruction in the aided Colleges of Bareilly, Agra, Lucknow, and Allahabad; but the impulse which the establishment of the College has given to education among the Muhammadans would cease, and the peculiar advantages attending a special residential College would be lost. It is very hopeful indication of success that the old students take a pride in their College, and, in the present crisis of its fate, are throwing their whole energies into the work of helping Mr Beck.

Hitherto the personality of Sir Syed Ahmad has completely overshadowed the Trustees. It is essential that the Governing Body should now come forward and re-organise the management. Apart from Mr Mahmud's peculiarities, there is a strong feeling among many Muhammadans against the action of Sir Syed Ahmad in attempting to hand over the College to his son as if it were a private inheritance. There is an equally strong objection to the institution being run as a proprietary College by Mr Beck, or any other European. It should belong to the Muhammadan community, and be managed by their best men. No one has yet come forward who will be accepted as fitted to discharge the functions of Sir Syed Ahmad. The Trustees are scattered all over India, but it is for them as the Governing Body to establish the College on principles other than that of the rule of a single man. Government may encourage them to do this, but I do not think it can assist them. In this matter the Muhammadan community must help itself, and rely on itself. My view is that at the annual meeting in December the Trustees should amend the constitution of the College. This they can do under the Regulations, and it is the best way of disposing of Mr Mahmud and the difficulties of administration. It seems the only way in which confidence in the stability of the College can be given to the Muhamadan community and to Government.

The financial difficulty is a separate thing. It was a mistake, in the present disorganized state of the internal management, to start subscription for fund for ten lakhs. It was also a mistake to talk of an University, and this ambitious talk has alienated the sympathies of many Muhammadan well-wishers. What is wanted is a Muhammadan College carried on the lines laid down by the founder, and this is all that for some generations the Muhammadans can hope to effect. The proper memorial to Sir Syed Ahmad was a subscription to discharge the liabilities of the College. Then comes re-organization; and thereafter if the Muhammadans are able to improve the working of the College; to take more students; to engage more professors; to raise the income from Rs. 70,000 to Rs. 1,00,000, well and good, but the time for this is not yet.

We have not yet obtained a clear and authentic statement of debts. I hope to have correct figure in July. Meanwhile I take Mr Beck's figure of Rs.60,000, about half of which is debenture debt. There is no reason why this debt should not be discharged, and I intended to press this point when I visited Aligarh. I intended to contribute myself, and I know of several Muhammadan gentlemen who are willing to contribute. I venture to submit for His Excellency's consideration that it is by aid in liquidating this debt that the sympathy of European well-wishers can best be manifested, and assistance from Government can most properly be given to the College. A contribution by the Viceroy himself will stimulate donations in a way that no amount of good advice could effect; and it would be to me a source of great satisfaction if I were able to read out in July a letter expressing His Excellency's approbation of the objects aimed at in the College, and urging on the Muhammadan community the importance of financial support.

I have known the College since it was founded, and I take a great interest in it. I have been three times stationed at Aligarh. The friendships and acquintanceship which I formed as` Assistant Collector were maintained and strengthened during the time I was Collector of the District, and during the last two months I have been visited by, and have talked over this question with, nearly every man of note in Aligarh and Bulandshahr.

On the subject of Government assistance I have consulted the Director of Public Instruction and the Financial Secretary to this Government. The Government grant to Aligarh was, in the year 1893, when an extra Professor was appointed, raised by Rs. 2,400. It is now Rs. 10,800 to the College, and Rs.6,000 to the School. The cost per scholar to public funds is:

	Rs	As
Aligarh College-	75	6
Bareilly College	72	0
Agra College	42	8

The cost to Aligarh College per scholar is Rs.295, so that Government contributes 25 per cent. I do not think that the yearly grant should be increased until at least the College is re-organized and placed on a stable basis.

As regards the grant of a lump sum, it will have been seen that I do not advocate a contribution to the Existing Fund. I think that the Muhammadans should themselves raise funds to improve their own College; but it would, I think, be legitimate as a recognition of the life work of Sir Syed Ahmad that Government should make grant in a lump sum to discharge the debentures. This would be about Rs.30,000. The College would save the interest now paid and the relief would be substantial

It is however, I fear, impossible to propose a grant from the Educational Budget of the Provinces. The whole of the money has been allotted, and any small savings are destined for Training Schools. This is the first year of the Provincial Contract. His Excellency knows that the Provinces last year were insolvent, and subsisted on the generosity of the Government of India.

The whole Provincial income has been allotted, except a portion which we were obliged to save in order to bring our balances up to the minimum. I cannot reduce Public Works grants. Expenditure on Plague has already far exceed the estimate, and this head of expenditure may involve an extra outlay. While, therefore, I should be glad if a grant from the Government could be made, I think that that if it is to be made, it should be made from Imperial Revenues, and in the name of the Government of India.

Yours sincerely,

(Sd) J.D.La Touche

52

From:

The Hon'ble Mr J.J.D.La Touche, C.S.I
Offg.Lieut.Governor of the N.W.P. and Oudh

To:

His Excellency The Earl of Elgin and Kincardine, G.M.S. etc.

Benares
July 10th, 1898

My Dear Lord Elgin,
I have sent to-day through Mr Babington Smith a copy of the Address which the Memorial Fund Committee proposes to present at Aligarh on 23rd July.

I remain

Dear Lord Elgin,

Yours sincerely

(Sd) La Touche

53

From: The Hon'ble Mr J.J.D.La Touche, C.S.I
Offg. Lieut. Governor of the N.W.P. and Oudh

To: H.Babington Smith, Esq., C.S.I
Private Secretary to the Viceroy

Benares;
July 10th,1898

My Dear Smith,
I enclose, for His Excellency's information, a copy of the Address which Sir Syed Ahmad Memorial Fund Committee propose to present

to me at Aligarh on 23rd instant. The wishes of the Committee under Section 4 of the Charitable Endowments Act VI of 1890, and Section 10 of the Act the securities would then be inalienable, except under the orders of Government. I have suggested this to Mr Beck.

Lord Elgin was good enough to think of writing a letter which I could read at the meeting on 23rd instant. I look upon such a letter as of the greatest value to the College in the present crisis of its fortunes, and I trust that I may receive it before the date fixed for my visit to Aligarh.

Yours sincerely
(sd) J.D.La Touche

P.S.-I also enclose a letter from Mr Beck to me, dated 5th July.

[Enclosure to the above letter]

54

From: Theodore Beck, Esq., B.A.
Principal, Mahomedan Anglo-Oriental College,
Aligarh

To; The Hon'ble Mr J.J.D.La Touche, C.S.I
Offg. Lieut.Governor of the N.W.P. and Oudh

Aligarh;
July 5th, 1898

My Dear Mr La Touche,
I send you a rough copy of the Address which the Memorial Committee proposes to read to you. It has been prepared by me in consultation with the President, Mohsin-ul-Mulk, and the Secretary, Aftab Ahmad Khan. I have written to Mahmood telling him not to prepare an Address on behalf of the Trustees without first ascertaining whether you want it, because I understand that your object in visiting the College is not to inspect the College and meet the trustees qua

Trustees, but to meet the Memorial Fund Committee. I very much doubt if the Trustees will be willing to sign an Address written by Mahmood. I wish to mention in confidence that it has been practically decided that Mahmood cannot be kept longer than the next Annual Meeting. What you said to me about the deterrent influence of Mahmood in getting subscriptions is quite true, except that a good many people have shown themselves willing to help us, more or less, on the understanding that measures will be taken in December. The great thing is to prevent interest dying out before that time. The Deputation to Lahore, headed by Mohsin-ul-Mulk, has had an excellent effect. The deputation visited only two towns and got Rs 18,000 promised. It will go the Punjab in the cold weather.

Mohsin-ul-Mulk has been working splendidly as the President of the Committee, to the considerable damage of his health, which is delicate. So has Aftab Ahmad. Mirza Abid Ali Beg has also proved himself a worker.

I wish to ask if you will very kindly not speak disparagingly of the University idea? It is through that that we have raised the money in the Punjab. We have explained clearly that by the University we simply mean to develop the College, so that some day in the future it may have a sufficiently strong staff to be able to confer its own degrees. All intelligent people know that this must be a distant ideal, possible not to be realised under two generations. If you prefer to say nothing about the University idea, we have no objection. But if you should discourage it, I fear it would have a depressing effect on our subscriptions. I hope you will excuse my making this suggestion.

We should be very glad if you would speak in Hindustani, your speech being of course published in English . A good many of the audience will not understand English.

A great many of our Old students are expected to be present. The occasion will be a great one. We hope to utilise it to inspire zeal in our old students.

I would suggest 8.A.M. on the 23rd as the time of the meeting, if that would suit you?

Our friend Denton, who has typhoid, shows some signs of improvement to-day. His temperature is rather low. I am glad to have rather better news of my wife also. We are expecting the auditor to-day. Another anxiety is that the Hyderabad people haven't sent their money since Sir Syed's death. I don't know why, so that I have great difficulty in paying the staff their salaries. However, with the exception of myself, I have managed to get them paid up-to-date. I trust the money will come in a few days. I fancy the hitch has occurred on technical grounds, which I think will now be removed.

I am sending you a copy of my annual report, in which I have attempted to show what is being done by the Mohammedans themselves.

May I have the pleasure of seeing you sometime on the 22nd or before the date of the meeting?

Yours sincerely

(SD) Theodore Beck.

55

From:

The Hon'ble Mr J.J.D.La Touche, C.S.I
Offg.Lieut.Governor of the N.W.P. and Oudh

To: His Excellency
The Earl of Elgin and Kincardine, G.M.S. etc.

Benares
July 10th, 1898

My Dear Lord Elgin,

I have sent to-day through Mr Babington Smith a copy of the Address which the Memorial Fund Committee propose to present at Aligarh on 23rd July. ---

I was pleased that in recommending a person for nomination on your Excellency's council, the non-official Members of this Council behaved with good sense. The Maharaja of Ajudhia and Raja Rampal Singh had both been eagerly canvassing, but in the result each had four votes out of eight, including his own. As neither would give way to the other, they agreed to unanimously recommend Nawab Faiyyaz Ali Khan. ... Faiyyaz Ali Khan is the son of Sir Faiz Ali Khan, K.C.S.I, deceased; he knows no English, but is an honourable, straightforward man, much respected. I am glad on the whole that a Mahomedan has been recommended for these provinces, and one who is not a vakil. Ajudhiya is head over ears in debt, and would spend lakhs in Calcutta. Raja Rampal Singh eats beef and drinks spirit and is not respected by the best class of Hindus. His notoriety is due to his Congress proclivities, though he is not clever enough to be a leader...

I remain
Dear Lord Elgin,
Yours sincerely
(Sd) La Touche

56

From : His Excellency
The Earl of Elgin and Kincardine, G.M.S. etc.

To: The Hon'ble Mr J.J.D.La Touche, C S.I
Offg. Lieut. Governor of the N.W.P. and Oudh

Viceregal Lodge,
Simla.
July 13th, 1898

Dear Mr La Touche,

I understand that you are about to visit Aligarh for the purpose of meeting the authorities of the Mahomedan Anglo-Oriental College, and the committee of the Syed Ahmed Memorial Fund; and I shall be greatly obliged if you will take this opportunity of expressing the interest which I feel in the prosperity of the College, and in the efforts which are being made to remove the temporary difficulties which have recently arisen.

In founding the Aligarh College Sir Syed Ahmed set before the Mahomedan community a high ideal of the objects at which education should aim. He endeavoured to provide not merely for instruction, but also for the formation of character, for the encouragement of the manly pursuits, for the promotion of a feeling of self-respect for the students, and for fostering among them an active sense of their duty as loyal subjects of the Queen Empress. In the attainment of these objects a great measure of success has been secured`; and I consider that it would be a misfortune of no small magnitude for the Mahomedan community, not only in he North-Western Provinces but throughout India, if the usefulness of the College were diminished, or the scope of its activity curtailed by the pressure of financial or administrative difficulties.

I have heard with pleasure that he Trustees of the College and many of its old pupils are exerting themselves in order to obtain funds for clearing of the existing debt, and for providing the means of placing the College upon a more stable basis. I trust that these efforts will be successful; and that Mahomedans in the first place, and also those who though not Mahomedans, feel the importance of furthering the education of Moslem youths upon the lines which I have described will not be backward in supporting this movement , and in thus paying a tribute of honour to the memory of the distinguished founder of the College.

I shall always consider myself fortunate in that I found an opportunity of visiting the College last year, when I had the privilege of making the acquaintance of Sir Syed Ahmed himself and of seeing the institution he loved so well under the inspiring influence of his presence. The remembrance of that day strengthens my desire to enrol myself among the friends of the College, and I should like to give practical expression to my sympathy by contributing the sum of

Rs.2,000 to the fund of which is now being raised. Perhaps you will kindly communicate this wish to mine to the committee.

I am
Yours very truly

(Sd.) Elgin.

57

From: His Excellency The Earl of Elgin and Kincardine, G.M.S.I.,&.c.

To: The Hon'ble Mr J.J.D.LaTaouche, C.S.I.,
Offg.Lieut.-Governor of the N.W.P. & Oudh

Viceregal Lodge
Simla,
July 13th, 1898

Dear Mr La Touche,
I have to thank you for your letter of 10th. It necessitates any alteration in the letter which I had already prepared and which accompanies this. When I saw Mr Beck here he assured me that the first purpose of any fund raised by the Committee would be to clear off any capital debt, and it seems to me that this clearly ought to be so. It bears so high a rate of interest that it is by far the most profitable investment that can be obtained, while there are obviously other advantages. I don't think, however, that I could usefully touch upon that, and I am sure the Committee will follow your advice. The idea of keeping the Fund quite separate from the College property was, I understood, primarily intended to get rid of any difficulties arising out of Mr Syed Mahmood's position; but, in any case, I should think there were advantages in it, if arrangements can be made so that the money subscribed is quite safe.

I shall be interested to hear the result of your Meeting.

I am inclined personally to hear to approve of the manner in which you propose to keep the modified plague resolutions in reserve. That we shall have to make modifications if plague attacks these large cities all admit, but we need not relax further than is expedient. The chief argument for action before an outbreak is, I think, that we may take the initiative, and shut out the possibility of its being said that we have given way and yielded to rioters what we would not to rational and peaceful representations. Therefore I think you and your officers should keep a finger on the pulse of the public feeling and act promptly, if occasion arises.

I am rather glad to hear of the election of a Mahomedan to the Viceroy's Council. Both Lord Lansdowne and I have had a great difficulty in getting satisfactory men to represent them. I always liked Pundit Bishambar Nath, though as an orator he was not lively!

Yours sincerely

(Sd) Elgin)

58

From: The Hon'ble Mr J.J.D.La Touche, C.S.I
Offg. Lieut. Governor of the N.W.P. and Oudh

To: His Excellency
The Earl of Elgin and Kincardine, G.M.S. etc.

Government House,
Allahabad
July 16th, 1898

My Dear Lord Elgin,
I am very proud to be bearer of your Excellency's letter on the Aligarh College Memorial Fund. The reading of it will, I feel sure, have an excellent effect, and I shall inform you of how our meeting goes off. I had a long talk to-day with Mr Mahmud. He is still staying in the Club at Allahabad, but seems fairly well at present, and has not the slightest intention of resigning. I shall say little or nothing, however, about the future management of the College. I go to meet the Memorial Fund Committee, not to visit the College as Lieutenant-Governor, or to hold an interview with the College authorities.

Yours sincerely

(Sd) J.D.La Touche

59

From: Theodore Beck, Esq., B.A.
Principal , Mahomedan Anglo-Oriental College,
Aligarh.

To: H.Babington Smith, Esq., C.S.I
Private Secretary to the Viceroy
Aligarh.
July 26th, 1898

My Dear H.B.,
I have been so rushed during the Lieutenant-Governor's visit that I have not had an opportunity before this writing to thank you for your kind letter. As to the Viceroy's subscription and even more his letter, I cannot tell you what I feel. He is the saviour of our College. The effect on the Mahomedans has been tremendous; I never knew such enthusiasm among them. We raised Rs. 18,500 in the meeting, and

one of the landlords of Aligarh, Ahmad Said Khan, one of the most straightforward and truthful men in his district, raised his subscription from one to five thousand after the meeting. The old students who were present held a meeting of their own afterwards, and promised Rs. 3,100, so that altogether the meeting brought us Rs.25,00, bringing up our total to Rs.86,000. It was only about Rs.30,000 when I saw you last. I am now trying to get Mahmood accept the post of President, with Mohsin-ul-Mulk as Secretary. If we can achieve this we shall stop all scandals and get out administrative difficulties.

I am afraid I may never have an opportunity of proving the feelings of personal devotion and gratitude to His Excellency for his extraordinary kindness. And I know, my dear H.B., how much we have to thank you too. I am so glad to hear that your marriage is to take place at Simla. Will you please convey to lady Elizabeth my feelings of regard and my heartfelt desire for her happiness.

La Touche has been awfully good to us. He took infinite trouble to heal up old differences, and his efforts are meeting with great success.

Ever yours sincerely

(Sd) Theodore Beck

60

From: The Hon'ble Mr J.J.D.La Touche, C.S.I
Offg.Lieut.Governor of the N.W.P. and Oudh

To: H.Babington Smith, Esq., C.S.I
Private Secretary to the Viceroy
Government House,
Naini Tal
July 27th, 1898

My Dear Smith,
I enclose a cutting from the *Pioneer* of 26th July which contains a report of the speech which I delivered at the Aligarh College. The meeting was, I think, a success. There was a very large assemblage, and a good deal of enthusiasm was exhibited. It was entirely in the direction of carrying out the policy of Sir Syed Ahmad. The party of retrogression is utterly discredited. Rs. 22,900 were subscribed in the hall. But besides the question of raising funds some solid progress has been made. I had an informal conference with the Trustees collectively, and most of the leading men came to discuss matters with me. I have now formally as Patron advised the Trustees on two points:

First, that they should offer to Mr Mahmud the office of Life President of the College instead of Life Secretary. Secondly, that they should appoint Nawab Mohsin-ul-Mulk as Secretary. The tenure of his appointment under Regulation 45 will be for three years.

These proposals will, I believe, be accepted by the Trustees, though if they did not get a lead they might never come to a conclusion.

They all agree that the chief administrative function of the College should be entrusted to a man in possession of full vigour of bodily and mental faculties. There is no doubt that the recent embezzlements would not have occurred had not the faculties of Sir Syed Ahmad been impaired by age. I have suggested that the duties of life President should be confined to presiding at meetings of the Trustees and directing the appointment of the European educational staff. Mr Mahmud will, I understand, offer no objection.

I agree with Mr Beck in thinking that Nawab Mohsin-ul-Mulk is the most capable man available. His views are in entire accord with the views of Government and the policy of Sir Syed Ahmad. The Trustees can not alter the Regulations till December, but it is important that the public should know that they have come to a decision. This will stop any canvassing for the office of the Secretary, and I have suggested to the Trustees that if they accept my advice they should now announce the course they intend to adopt on these two points. It will be material assistance to the efforts now being made to collect funds.

I also tried to effect a reconciliation between the faction of Sami Ullah Khan and the College authorities. Sami Ullah Khan and the other malcontents who refused the office of Trustee in 1896 have written to Mr Mahmud withdrawing their previous letters, assuring him and the Trustees of their desire to help the College in every way in their power, and hoping that the old disputes may be buried. This is entirely in accordance with the general wish of the Trustees. I do not think Sami Ullah Khan should be appointed Trustee at present, but he can do the College good a great deal of harm if he stands aloof, and he really, I believe, wishes to help, and can do so. Mohsin-ul-Mulk promised me, indeed offered, to put Sami Ullah Khan at once on the Memorial Fund Committee, and both will go on a deputation to Rampur, whence they expect a substantial contribution.

Mahmud may write an insulting reply to Sami Ullah Khan's letter, which I handed personally to Mohsin-ul-Mulk . But I hope not; and if Mahmud will say that he accepts the proffered aid, there will remain no division among the Mahomedans, the Syed's policy as approved by Government will be established, Mohsin-ul-Mulk will be appointed Secretary, and Sami Ullah Khan and his party will have an opportunity of showing by their acts that they are true friends of the College as they profess to be.

Yours sincerely

(Sd) J.D.La Touche

61

From: The Hon'ble Mr J.J.D.La Touche, C.S.I
Offg.Lieut.Governor of the N.W.P. and Oudh

To: H.Babington Smith, Esq., C.S.I
Private Secretary to the Viceroy

Government House,
Naini Tal.
July 28th, 1898

My Dear Smith,
In continuation of my letter of yesterday, I enclose, for His Excellency's information, copy of the reply of Mr Mahmud to the letter of reconciliation sent by Sami Ullah Khan to him. It is in every way satisfactory. Mahmud has by his kindly and generous words healed his old dispute, and the friends of the College now present a united front to all the detractors. The policy of Sir Syed Ahmed Khan has triumphed all along the line, and the enemies of the College can only prosper when there are divisions among the friends of the College.

As a token of the reconciliation Sami Ullah Khan will accompany a deputation to Rampur.

Yours sincerely

(Sd) J.D. La Touche

[Enclosed the above letter]

62

From: The Hon'ble Syed Mahmood,
Life Honorary Secretary of the Mahomedan Anglo-Oriental College,
Aligarh

To: Maulvi Sami Ullah Khan Sahib, C.M.G.
Kunwar Lutf Ali Khan Sahib
Khwajah Mohamed Yusuf Sahib

Aligarh
July 25th, 1898

Dear Sirs,
I acknowledge with much pleasure the receipt of your letter dated Aligarh, July 24, 1898. I am very glad to hear that you are anxious to assist in our task of raising the Syed Ahmad Memorial Fund and thus helping the great national work the foundations of which were laid by my late respected and beloved father, Sir Syed Ahmad Khan, K.C.S.I, LL, D, but which is yet very far from completion. I feel personally very grateful to tell those well-wishers of the Mahomedan community and admirers of my late father who have taken in hand the task of raising a worthy memorial to his memory, which shall place the College to which he devoted the latter part of his life on a firm and secure basis, and above all to His Excellency Lord Elgin, Viceroy and Governor-General of India, to His Honour Sir Antony MacDonnell, Lieutenant-Governor of the North-Western Provinces and Oudh, and to the Honble J.D. LaTouche, C.S.I, Lieutenant Governor of the North-West Provinces and Oudh, not only for their munificent personal donations to the fund, but still more for the extreme kindness they have shown by word and deed. When the representative of the Government of Her Most Gracious Majesty the Queen have shown such interest and sympathy in our work we cannot but feel our zeal, as Mohomaedans, stimulated for disinterested efforts for the common good. I am very glad to join with you in forgetting any misunderstandings that may have taken place in the past, and I trust now that all of us, Mohomedans, will give proof of a

spirit of self-help, of patriotic feeling for our community, and of loyalty to our benign Government, the result of which will be that the plant which my father fostered in his tender years will grow into a magnificent tree, and that future generations of the Mohomedans will enjoy the advantages of a great seat of learning and civilisation similar to the English Universities of Oxford and Cambridge, which was the original aim that he had in view.

With many thanks for your expression of good-will,

I have the honour to be, Sirs,

Yours most obedient Servant

Syed Mahmood

63

From: H.Babington Smith, Esq. C.S.I
Private Secretary to the Viceroy

To: H.H. The Lieut.-Governor of the N.W.P and Oudh

Lieutenant Governor's Camp.
Viceregal Lodge,
Simla;
July 30th,1898

Dear Mr La Touche,
The Viceroy has been much interested in reading your letter to me of the 27th and 28th instant, and he desires me to congratulate you on the successful result of your exertions. The outcome appears to His Excellency to be satisfactory in every way, both as regards the financial position of the College, and especially, in the more difficult

matter of restoring concord among the conflicting elements concerned.

If you have an opportunity, and if you think it desirable to do so His Excellency would be glad if you would express to Syed Mahmood his satisfaction in hearing of the manner in which he has contributed towards the healing of the breach.

I hope that the crisis may now be considered to be past, and that the College is in smooth water again.

If the *Pioneer* is correct in saying that an estate worth 3 lakhs has been contributed to the Fund, they would be placed in a thoroughly sound financial position.

Yours sincerely

(Sd) H.Babington Smith

64

From: The Hon'ble Mr J. J . D. La Touche, C.S.I
Offg.Lieut.Governor of the N.W.P. and Oudh

To: H.Babington Smith, Esq., C.S.I
Private Secretary to the Viceroy

Government House,
Naini Tal.
July 30th, 1898

My Dear Smith,
I have received telegrams from Nawab Mohsin-ul-Mulk and Maulvi Sami Ullah Khan, members of the Deputation that visited Rampur on behalf of the Aligarh College. They announce the result of their

application to the Nawab of Rampur. He has given a donation of Rs. 50,000, and has increased his monthly grant from Rs. 100 to Rs.200. This is very handsome, and the financial safety of the College is assured, even if other Mahommedan Chiefs do not follow the example.

Yours sincerely

(Sd) J.D. La Touche

65

From : His Excellency
The Earl of Elgin and Kincardine, G.M.S. etc

To: The Hon'ble Mr J.J.D.La Touche, C.S.I
Offg.Lieut.Governor of the N.W.P. and Oudh

Viceregal Lodge,
Simla;
July 13th,1898

Dear Mr La Touche,
I understand that you are about to visit Aligarh for the purpose of meeting the authorities of the Mahomedan Anglo-Oriental College, and the committee of the Syed Ahmed Memorial Fund; and I shall be greatly obliged if you will take this opportunity of expressing the interest which I feel in the prosperity of the College, and in the efforts which are being made to remove the temporary difficulties which have recently arisen.

In founding the Aligarh College Sir Syed Ahmed set before the Mahomedan community a high ideal of the objects at which education should aim. He endeavoured to provide not merely for instruction, but also for the formation of character, for the encouragement of the manly pursuits, for the promotion of a feeling of self -respect for the students, and for fostering among them an active sense of their duty as loyal subjects of the Queen Empress. In the attainment of these objects a great measure of success has been secured`; and I consider that it would be a misfortune of no small magnitude for the Mahomedan community, not only in he North-Western Provinces but throughout India, if the usefulness of the College were diminished , or the scope of its activity curtailed by the pressure of financial or administrative difficulties.

I have heard with pleasure that he Trustees of the College and many of its old pupils are exerting themselves in order to obtain funds for clearing of the existing debt, and for providing the means of placing the College upon a more stable basis. I trust that these efforts will be successful; and that Mahomedans in the first place, and also those who, though not Mahomedans, feel the importance of furthering the education of Moslem youths upon the lines which I have described, will not be backward in supporting this movement, and in thus paying a tribute of honour to the memory of the distinguished founder of the College.

I shall always consider myself fortunate in that I found an opportunity of visiting the College last year, when I had the privilege of making the acquaintance of Sir Syed Ahmed himself and of seeing the institution he loved so well under the inspiring influence of his presence. The remembrance of that day strengthens my desire to enrol myself among the friends of the College, and I should like to give practical expression to my sympathy by contributing the sum of Rs 2,000 to the fund of which is now being raised. Perhaps you will kindly communicate this wish to mine to the committee.

I am

Yours very truly

(Sd.) Elgin.

66

From: H.Babington Smith, Esq., C.S.I
Private Secretary to the Viceroy

To: H.H. The Lieut -Governor of the N.W.P and Oudh
Lieutenant Governor's Camp.

Viceregal Lodge,
Simla.
July 30th, 1898

Dear Mr La Touche,
The Viceroy has been much interested in reading your letter to me of the 27th and 28th instant, and he desires me to congratulate you on the successful result of your exertions. The outcome appears to His Excellency to be satisfactory in every way, both as regards the financial position of the College, and especially, in the more difficult matter of restoring concord among the conflicting elements concerned.

If you have an opportunity, and if you think it desirable to do so His Excellency would be glad if you would express to Syed Mahmood his satisfaction in hearing of the manner in which he has contributed towards the healing of the breach.

I hope that the crisis may now be considered to be past, and that the College is in smooth water again.

If the *Pioneer* is correct in saying that an estate worth 3 lakhs has been contributed to the Fund, they would be placed in a thoroughly sound financial position.

Yours sincerely
(Sd) H.Babington Smith

PERSONAL

67

From: Sir J. Strachey

To: Lord Lytton

1st August, 1877

My Dear Lytton,
I forgot to tell you about the telegram from Bradford, which you gave me last night, about the Turkish Envoy

I suppose we are to understand from it that the Council does not favour the idea of attaching Syud Ahmed Khan to the Mission, and I think that after the Secretary of State updated you were not much disposed to press the plan unless the Council would himself take it up in learning what Bradford had to say.

If you think it unlikely that Syud Ahmed will be wanted it would be as well to issue at once the orders about the Committee on Provincial Public Works arrangements of which Colvin is to be President. For the only case for delay has been the doubt whether it would not be necessary to send Colvin down to Allygurh.

Col. Williams told me the other day that there were questions regarding Provincial P.W. establishment .

68

From: John Strachey

To: Lord Lytton

17 November, 1877.

I sent to you yesterday my letter about salt. There are several other matters that I ought to have written to you about, but I have been travelling so constantly that both spirit and flesh have been weak.

I think moreover there is really only one subject regarding which I have anything to say of immediate importance. I have heard by telegraph, that Syud Ahmed went off to Delhi to see the Turkish Envoy. Whether he actually saw him, and what the result was, I do not yet know.

I have now written to Syud Ahmed to the effect that I am not myself going to Allyghur, and that therefore can hardly manage to see him , but that he will no doubt have an opportunity of seeing Burne and Aitchison and that I hope he will communicate to them any information of interest which he has been able to get. I dare say that Bradfaord has in part learnt already which Syud Ahmed may have had to tell, but as I myself can not go to see him, I think it would please him if Burne or Aitchison would talk to him on the subject. Otherwise he might possibly think that he has been slighted. If you approved I have no doubt that he could go easily to Agra while you are there, and he has so constantly been in the habit of paying his respects to Viceroys and lesser persons that his visit would lead to no suspicion. Perhaps you could tell Burne to communicate your wishes to Syud Ahmed whatever they may be. In my first letter to Syud Ahmed asking him to go to Delhi I said that I hoped he could let me know what his expenses were and I added that possibly it might be necessary for him to spend a little money on trifling presents of ceremony etc. and that I hoped he could let me reimburse any such charges. If Burne or Aitchison see him perhaps they will settle this business in a delicate way.

I do not think I have ever told you how much I admired your telegram to Lord Salisbury, and his reply about broad-gauge...

I hope to be at Allahabad on the 21th and at Calcutta on the 27th. We were glad to learn that you were having such a pleasant journey. I shall not be sorry to get back to a civilised house in Calcutta.

Believe me
My dear Lytton
Yours

John Strachey

69

17 July 1879

My Dear Lytton

I think that the enclosed letter from Bernard and its accompaniments will show you clearly how the question of the Oudh Judgeship stands. I think it could be quite enough if Syud Mahmud had one the lowest grade of Judgeship on Rs 1333 a month.

John Strachey

70

27 February 1879

Dear Sir John,
The facts about the Oudh Judicial Scheme are set out in the enclosed draft letter which I am today submitting to Sir Alex Arbuthnot for approval.

There are besides sub-judgeships and Moonsifships, four new judgeships.

1 on 1833 Rs a month.

1 on 1666 Rs a month.

2 on 1333 Rs a month.

The sub-judgeship carries salaries of 500 Rs to 800 Rs. The two Mysore men are to be given salaries of Rs 600 and Rs 500 respectively. So their transfer to Oudh can not interfere with the appointment of Mahmood to one of the new judgeships.

The appointment letter as submitted to Sir Alexander distinctly says that one appointment of the judgeship should be given to a native.

Mahmood has gone to Europe, promising to be back by May next I had H.E. The Viceroy's permission to tell him that, so far as His Excellency was concerned this short absence from India would not effect his chance of being recommended for one of these judgeships.

I am
Yours sincerely

C. Bernard

APPENDIX

The Bill

A Bill to make better provision for the Constitution of the Council of the Governor General of India and for amending the Legislative Councils of the several Presidencies and Provinces of India by enlarging their number, constituting them on partial Elective basis, and increasing their powers.

The Petition

To The Honourable The Commons of the United Kingdom of Great Britain and Ireland in Parliament Assembled.

The Humble petition of the undersigned Indian Mahomedans:

Shewth. - That your petitioners pray that your Honourable House will not introduce the principle of election into the Constitution of the Indian councils, as requested by the Indian National Congress.

That your petitioners believe that the effects of introducing this principle would be to destroy that that enhanced justice which has been hitherto the basis of British Rule and would place them and other minorities in an almost intolerable subjection to classes actively hostile to their welfare.

Your petitioners beg to lay before you the following facts:

1. That the Indian Mahomedans, although only one-fifth of the inhabitants of India, are the largest single community and number not less than 50,000,000 souls: and that therefore the welfare of so large a number of Her Majesty's subjects cannot be an object of indifference to you Honourable House.

2. That through its history, traditions, bravery and intelligence the Indian Mahomedan nation is a factor of great importance in Indian politics.

3. That in as much as the Indian Mahomedans are not confined, like the nationalities of Europe, to any special locality, but are dispersed throughout India among the multitude of other races and castes inhabiting the continent, they are in most parts of India in a considerable minority: and that therefore in any system of election they must of necessity be outvoted. Overwhelming proof of this is furnished by the existing municipalities. It may be safely said that in the event of a popular agitation appealing to the religious sentiments of the people, such for example as the agitation now afloat to prohibit cow-killing, a measure that would deprive the poor Mahomedans of one of their most important articles of food, scarcely a single Mahomedan member representing Mahomedan sentiment could be returned.

4. That the demand for the introduction of an elective system into the Government of India proceeds from the class of English-educated Hindus, a class that is exceptionally well able to make its voice heard both in England and in India; while the Mahomedans, being very backward in English education, have been unable to give equal prominence to their views. And therefore, that your Honourable Home should not be led into supposing by the amount of noise and stir produced by the National Congress Party that the quantity and quality of native opinion opposed to it is insignificant or uninfluential.

5. That any system of proportionate representation would in no way protect Mahomedan interests, inasmuch as the Hindus of various races would be in a majority of four to one, and as all matters in the Council would be decided by a simple majority, the Mahomedan members would always be inevitably outvoted.

That your petitioners pray that your Honourable House will retain the principle of nomination by the Government of all members of the Indian Councils, by which alone their interests and the interests of their minorities can be protected.

That your petitioners confidently rely on receiving from your Honourable House a full and complete consideration of their case.

And your petitioners will ever pray.

The Statement about the Signatures to the Petition issued by the Secretary of the United Indian Patriotic Association.

The places from which signatures have been obtained are given below, together with the number of signatures received from each place. When signatures have been received from two or more towns or villages in one district they will be grouped under the chief town of then district, consequently the names must be understood to refer to districts rather than towns.

Delhi (Punjab)	4,183
Aligarh (NWP)	2,817
Lahore (Punjab)	2,223
Allahabad (NWP)	1,959
Moradabad (NWP)	1,745
Batala (Punjab)	1,613
Lucknow (Oudh)	1,521
Agra (NWP)	1,503
Cawnpore (NWP)	1,304
Eta (NWP)	1181

Fategarh (NWP)	1125
Ghazipur (NWP)	1112
Ferozpur (Punjab)	1080
Gujrat (Punjab)	914
Muzuffernagar (NWP)	907
Ajmere (Rajputana)	784
Muttra (NWP)	771
Jaunpur (NWP)	752
Bijnor (NWP)	717
Mymensingh (Bengal)	693
Calcutta (Bengal)	577
Patna (Bengal)	445
Meerut (NWP)	314
Sandhila (Oudh)	309
Rewari (Punjab)	308
Azamgarh (NWP)	281
Hyderabad (Sind)	230
Nagpur (Central Provinces)	226
Bulandshahr (NWP)	226
Budaon (NWP)	217

Jullundur (Punjab)	195
Hoshiarpur (Punjab)	192
Umballa (Punjab)	187
Durbhunga (Bengal)	173
Panipat (Punjab)	172
Kasur (Punjab)	170
Kurnal (Punjab)	169
Rangpore (Bengal)	164
Karachi (Sind)	148
Monghyr (Bengal)	144
Jessore (Bengal)	142
Sherkot (Sind)	131
Pandua (Bengal)	127
Bhopal (Rajputana)	125
Sewan (Bengal)	125
Mainipuri (NWP)	125
Shikarpur (Sind)	124
Mandawar (Mysore)	114
Maisinghpur	91
Mozaffargarh (Punjab)	90
Dinapore (Bengal)	86

Indore (Rajputana)	83
Sukkur (Sind)	81
Tumkur (Madras)	80
Rohtak (Punjab)	67
Bilgram (Oudh)	67
Dindigul (Madras)	63
Baghwanpura (Punjab)	63
Fatehpur (NWP)	59
Chapra (Bengal)	55
Barabanki (Oudh)	54
Dumkal	48
Hugli (Bengal)	41
Unao (Oudh)	39
Bareilly (NWP)	38
Partabgarh (Oudh)	26
Jubbulpore (Central Provinces)	22
Surat (Bombay)	19
Muzufferpur (Bengal)	13
Midnapur (Bengal)	157
Total:	**29,299**

The above signatures include many men of influence and weight in the Mahomedan community. An analysis of 4,568 signatures show the following result as regards the profession and occupations of the signatories: -

Zamindars	1,068
Trade	643
Service	637
Shopkeepers	563
Students	281
Workmen	151
Cultivators	113
Medical Men	75
Priests	69
Teachers	65
Legal Profession	48
Govt. Pensioners	35
Miscellaneous	316
Unspecified	505

Biographical Notes

1. **Abdul Lateef, Nawab** (1824-1893) was the founder, Secretary of the Mohamedan Literary Society, the earliest Association formed by the Muslims of India which he founded in 1863. It was the earliest educational and political association of the Muslims established for the purpose of representing their views throughout the country and promoting the growth of an inclination on the part of the rising generation of Muslims to share the benefits of education and the means of general progress held out by the British government.

Sir Syed visited Ghazipur as a guest of Nawab Abdul Lateef and attended the six monthly meeting of the Mohemadan Literary Society on 6 October 1863 and delivered an exquisite lecture in Persian on patriotism and the necessity of promoting knowledge in India. Nawab Abdul Lateef was "the pioneer of Muslim renaissance in Bengal, if not in India".

2. **Ajoodhia Nath, Pandit (1840-1892).** A Kashmiri Brahman, was educated at Agra College; joined the Bar in 1862 and became Professor of law at Agra in 1869; very successful as a pleader and amassed a fortune; a scholar of Persian and Arabic he became member of the N.W.P. Legislative Council; joined the Indian National Congress in 1888 and became President of Allahabad Standing Congress Committee; later became Joint General Secretary of I.N.C.

3. **Ardagh, Sir John Charles** (1840-1907) Private Secretary to the Marquess of Lansdowne, Governor-General and Viceroy, from Dec. 1888 - Jan.1894 and later to Earl of Elgin, Viceroy and Governor-General of India, from January to April 1894.

4. **Babibgton Smith, Sir Henry** (1863 - 1923) Principal Private Secretary to Chancellor of Exchequer, 1891 - 92; Private Secretary to Lord Elgin, the Viceroy and Governor-General of India.

5. **Beck, Theodore** (1859-1899); Educated at a Quaker school, and later at University of London and Trinity College Cambridge; appointed Principal of the M.A.O. College, Aligarh, when he was only 24.; played a crucial rule in the establishment and running of the College. He died at a comparatively young age at Simla on 2 September 1899.

6. **Bernard, Sir Charles Edward** (1837-1901). I.C.S.; began his service in the Punjab in 1858; was Secretary to the Bengal Government, 1871-1875; Secretary to Sir Richard Temple on his famine mission to Madras and Bombay in 1877; Home Secretary to the Government of India, 1878-1880; retired and returned to England in 1886 and was appointed Secretary in the Revenue and Statistics Department of the India Office.

7. **Elgin, Victor Alexander Bruce**, 9th Earl of Elgin and Kincardine (1849- 1917); son of the 8th Earl of Elgin and Viceroy of India, 1862 - 63; was himself Viceroy and Governor-General of India, 1894-1899.

8. **Gorst Right Hon. Sir John Elden** (1835-1916) Under Secretary of State for India, 1886 -1891; M.P. for Cambridge and Chatham, 1886 - 1892; M.P. for Cambridge University from 1893 onward.

9. **Hamilton, Lord George Frances** (1845- 1927); Under Secretary of State for India, 1874-78; Vice President of Council, 1878-80; Secretary of State for India, 1895-1903.

10. **La Touche, Sir James John Digges** (1844 -1921)
Joined the Civil Service in the N.W.P. , 1867; Member of the Legislative Council, N.W.P, 1891; Chief Secretary, 1893; Additional Member of the Governor-General's Legislative Council; Officiating Lieutenant-Governor of N.W.P., 1898; Lieutenant-Governor of Agra and Oudh, 1901- 07; Member of the Council of India, 1907-1914.

11. Lansdowne, Henry Charles Keith Petty-FitzMaurice, Fifth Marquess of (1845-1927). Became Under Secretary for India in 1880 and Viceroy and Governor-General of India, 1889-1894. During his period the Legislative Councils were reconstituted and its members were given the rights of financial discussion. He also founded the Imperial Library and the Record Office in India. In 1895 he returned to England and was appointed Secretary of War and in 1900 became Foreign Secretary of Great Britain.

12. Lytton, Edward Robert Bulwer, First Earl of (1831-1891). Before his appointment as the Viceroy and Governor-General of India, 1876-1880 he had been the British Attaché at the Hague, St. Petersburg, Constantinople and Vienna; the main events during his viceroyalty were the Afghan War, 1879-180 and the famines in Bombay, Madras and Mysore; he also introduced the Vernacular Press Act.

13. MacDonnell, Sir Antony Patrick (1844 -1925) I.C.S. Acting Lieutenant-Governor of Bengal, 1893; Member of the Supreme Council, 1893 -95; Lieutenant-Governor of N.W.P., 1895 -1901; Member of the Council of India, 1902.

14. **Muhsin al-Mulk, Nawab Mahdi Ali Khan** (1837-1907) was born at Atawa; educated in traditional Islamic madrasas; started his career as a clerk and rose to the post of Tahsildar; became Deputy Collector in 1867; was appointed Inspector General of Revenue of Hyderabad State in 1871; after his retirement in 1893 came to Aligarh and was appointed Secretary to Board of Trustees. He was the founder member of All India Muslim League.

15. **Muir, Sir William**. (1819 - 1905). I.C.S. Entered the Bengal Civil Service, 1837; Secretary to N.W.P Government, 1852; Member of the Board of Revenue, N.W.P, 1856; during the Mutiny was in charge of the Intelligence Department, Agra; Member of the Governor-General's Legislative Council, 1864; Secretary to the Government of India, in the Foreign Department, 1865; Member of the Supreme Council, 1868; Lieutenant-Governor, N.W.P., 1868 - 1874; Finance Minister to the Supreme Council, 1874 -76; Member of the Council of India, 1876 - 85; Principal and Vice-chancellor of

Edinburgh University, 1885-1902; author of *Life of Mahomed*, *Annals of early Caliphate*, *The Koran*, etc.

16. Sham Bihari Lal, a Head Clerk in Sir Syed's Office since June 1883. Sir Syed had employed him because of his family background but was unaware of his previous conviction for embezzlement while in the service of Punjab Government. Over the years he was able to embezzle 1,05409 Rs. from the College fund. The theft was discovered by Sir Syed in July 1895. Sham Bihari Lal later committed suicide in prison. Sir Syed died three years later with a broken heart because of this affair.

17. Siva Prasad, The Hon'ble Raja (1823-1895), of Benares Was educated at Benares College and became a Vakil of Maharaja of Baharatpur, later appointed Naib Mir Munshi of William Edwards; Under Secretary in the Foreign Department; Mir Munshi in the Benares Agency; Joint Inspector in the Department of Public Instructions and in 1860 Inspector of Schools. He was, in 1883, a Member of the Governor General's Legislative Council. He is the author of 32 books, 18 in Hindi and the rest in Urdu.

18. Strachey, Lieutenant-General Sir Richard (1817-1908**;** Secretary to Sir John Peter Grant, Governor of Central Provinces, 1857. In 1869 he was appointed a member of the Governor-General's Council. He returned to England in 1871 and was appointed Inspector of Railways in the India Office. After his retirement in 1875 he was made a Member of the Council of India. He returned to India in 1878 to preside over the Famine Commission, 1878-1879. After his retirement in 1875 he was made a Member of the Council of India. He returned to India in 1878 to preside over the Famine Commission, 1878-1879.

19. Strachey, Sir John (1823-1907); went to India in 1842; served in the N.W.P; was Judicial Commissioner in C.P., 1862; Officiating Chief Commissioner of Oudh, 1866-67; Member of the Governor-General's Supreme Council, 1868-1872; Lieutenant-Governor of the N.W.P., 1874-1876; Financial Member of the Supreme Council, 1876-1880; Member of the Council for India, 1885-1895.

20. Temple, Sir Richard 1826-1902); author of a number of books on India, including the famous, *Legends of the Punjab.* He was Secretary to the Chief Commissioner of the Punjab, 1854; Chief Commissioner of the Central Provinces, 1862; Financial Member of the Governor General's Council, 1868; Lieutenant-Governor of Bengal, 1874 to 1877; Governor of Bombay, 1877, and finally after returning to England in 1880 became M.P. for the Evesham Division of Worcestershire, 1885-92, and Kingston, Surrey, 1892-95.

INDEX

A

B

C

D

E

F

G

H

I

J

K

L

M

T

Z